W9-CXA-057

INTEGRATING PSYCHOLOGY AND THEOLOGY

Elbows Together but Hearts Apart

Kirk E. Farnsworth

UNIVERSITY
PRESS OF
AMERICA

Copyright © 1981 by

University Press of America, Inc.

P.O. Box 19101, Washington, D.C. 20036

Library of Congress Cataloging in Publication Data

Farnsworth, Kirk E.
   Integrating psychology and theology.

   Includes index.
   1. Christianity--Psychology. I. Title.
BR110.F37   201'.9   81-40100
ISBN 0-8191-1851-6   AACR2
ISBN 0-8191-1852-4 (pbk.)

To

Sharon, who sees God in the darkness,
who sings to His glory but does not
hide Him with words

Jim, whose integration begins before
he thinks about it, who embodies
what he believes

Contents

Preface   vii

CHAPTER I: CONCEPTUAL RELATION   1
Models 3
    Credibility Model — Conformability Model —
    Convertibility Model — Compatibility Model —
    Complementarity Model
Notes 9

CHAPTER II: EMBODIED INTEGRATION   11
Humanness 12
Knowing Truth 13
    Parameters for Knowing Truth — Types of Truth
Notes 21

CHAPTER III: A PSYCHOLOGICAL BASIS FOR INTEGRATION   23
Conduct of Inquiry 27
    Mentality — Motive — Method
Notes 38

CHAPTER IV: A THEOLOGICAL BASIS FOR INTEGRATION   43
Conduct of Inquiry 45
    Mentality — Motive — Method
Notes 54

CHAPTER V: AN ANTHROPOLOGICAL BASIS FOR INTEGRATION   59
Terminology 60
    Body — Mind — Soul — Spirit — Heart
Human-Divine Encounter 65
    Indwelling — Faith — Prayer
Notes 72

Epilogue   77
Note 78

Author Index   79

Subject Index   81

Preface

Living as God is calling me, as a Christian and as a psychologist, I wonder at times about the amount of writing being done on the subject these days. I wonder to what extent people are living what they are writing. It seems to me it would be fairly easy to write about a Christian view of psychology, or about a psychological view of Christianity, but would it be true to life? Would it be true to how I live psychologically and as a Christian? I think the answer to that is in the living, not the writing.

The emphasis of this book is on living with, not on writing about; on living with God, not on writing about God; on knowing God's truths, not on knowing about God's truths. It is more on what happens "in here" than on what happens "out there". I think this is the key issue of integration: is it done "in here", in my life, or "out there", in other people's lives? Do I give testimony to what God is actually doing in my life, to what I personally *know*, or do I simply review what God is apparently doing in other people's lives, what I generally *know about*?

A bill of fare with one real raisin on it instead of the word "raisin", with one real egg instead of the word "egg", might be an inadequate meal, but it would at least be a commencement of reality. The contention . . . that we ought to stick to non-personal elements exclusively seems like saying that we ought to be satisfied forever with reading the naked bill of fare. I think, therefore, that however particular questions connected with our individual destinies may be answered, it is only by acknowledging them as genuine questions, and living in the sphere of thought which they open up, that we become profound.[1]

The in-here/out-there problem takes three forms. The first is related to the common assumption that all truth is God's truth. If that is true, then knowing God's truths through psychological and theological inquiries involves living with God. It follows, then, that God must somehow be active in the entirety of both inquiries. That is a real problem, though, particularly in psychological inquiry. The *modus operandi* is to leave God "out there" during the data-collection phase of psychological research. It is assumed that the Christian psychologist need only maintain his/her scientific and Christian standards of intellectual honesty and personal integrity in doing the research and applying the conclusions of the research. And then, since God's creation is ordered, integration is assumed possible because psychology and theology both investigate the same created, ordered universe. God's place, particularly on the psychological side of all that, is simply a passive cause for agreement: He is expected to be active only in upholding the objects of psychological inquiry.

Perhaps God is also involved by design through a prayerful concern for ethical psychological research methods and applications of results, but He is not expected to take an active part in the methodology itself — through the activity of the Holy Spirit in each human participant's experience during the experiment — to aid in the generating of the information leading to those results. In short, Christian psychologists limit God's activity in revealing His truth to both ends of the research process, severely restricting His involvement in the middle.

A second problem concerns how integration is done "in here". Attempts at integration frequently appear to simply be mental exercises of conceptually relating similar conclusions of two disciplines. Read something in a psychology text, find a similar statement in a theology text, and there you have it — the beginnings of a Christian psychology. That is interesting, but it is not integration. Living out its implications in my life over time — bringing it "in here" — is missing. Helmut Thielicke says it well in his advice to young seminary students, pointing out the deficiency ". . . of a merely conceptual experience. Some truth or other has not been 'passed through' as a primary experience, but has been replaced by 'perception' of the literary or intellectual deposit of what another's primary experience . . . has discovered. Thus one lives at second hand."[2]

A variation on looking for concepts that actually are similar is finding two that are not, and manipulating them so they will fit. One could end up with two shadows connected to no substance! Clark Pinnock makes a similar point in his review of Francis Schaeffer's book/film *How Should We Then Live?* He concludes that

> lining up visible historical events with their visible spiritual causes is not easy even in exhaustive studies, and Schaeffer's claim to be doing that in this slender book and on this scale is ludicrous. The pretentiousness of the effort will return to haunt him . . . . [Also,] there is some indication here that Schaeffer, like the old liberals, has sacrificed authentically biblical themes to some ideas of his own because of the requirements of his apologetic argument. For all his desire to be true to the Bible, he has a tendency to tailor its message to his system.[3]

More shadow than substance.

It is interesting, however, to compare the writing with the living, the book with L'Abri. "Ironically, there is political wisdom in Schaeffer, not in his book, but in his community, L'Abri, which consciously and effectively strives to be an alternative society, a city on the hill, the embodiment in history of the social truth of the coming kingdom."[4]

The third problem concerns integration itself. Even though most "integration" being done today is seemingly not "in here", it certainly is "in". Integration has become a popular pastime and a burgeoning business.[5] It is easy to forget, I think, that integration itself should not be the focus. That again, is "out there". Integration does not deserve the ontic dignity and status it so often receives.[6] Knowing God, "in here", does. "The Lord says: Let not the wise man bask in his wisdom, nor the mighty man in his might, nor the rich man in his riches. Let them boast in this alone: That they truly know me, and that I am the Lord of justice and of righteousness whose love is steadfast; and that I love to be this way."[7]

Living with the Lord of justice and righteousness is what legitimizes integration. It is what makes integration a reality for me. And it involves every area of my life — whether I am reading Scripture, learning with my wife, Rosie, how to live simply so that others might simply live, or standing up in the garden on a hot summer day to feel the cool breeze that comes by every few minutes. God's truth is everywhere.

A final word, not of apology but for clarity, about what I am trying to accomplish with this book. My agenda is twofold. First, I want to make an original contribution to the restructuring of the discipline of psychology to make possible what I would regard as a truly Christian (Spirit-filled) psychology. I have no illusions, however, that what I have come up with — a humanistic, phenomenological, human science psychology — is the only alternative or is anything more than a beginning. If the reader is uncomfortable with this direction, then at least I am reasonably sure that as a thread running throughout the book, it holds together the diversity of ideas that would otherwise be disconnected.

That reveals my second purpose, to present a wide variety of discoveries I have made regarding such things as how I can know truth, the nature of the Bible and what reading it entails, who/what I am as a person, and how I might live more fully in the presence of God. My hope is that any dissatisfaction the reader may have with my first purpose, describing my view of psychology, will not prevent him or her from being stimulated and encouraged by my second purpose, presenting my view of human-divine encounter. Or vice versa.

I want to thank the senior seminar Trinity College students, whom I deeply appreciate for stimulating me to pursue and articulate ever more clearly the ideas contained in this book. And especially my son, Craig, for his creative, precise graphic illustrations of many of those ideas throughout the book. I also appreciate being given permission by the author to use the extended quote from Peter A. Bertocci, *Free Will, Responsibility, and Grace* (New York: Abingdon, 1957), and by the publisher to quote the material from Richard J. Foster, *Celebration of Discipline: The Path to Spiritual Growth* (New York: Harper & Row, 1978). Finally, I want to thank my colleagues, several of whom appear in the footnotes, for their vigorous interaction and patient understanding. I hope this book will encourage each of us and many others to seek first God's kingdom and His righteousness "in here", all to God's glory.

Kirk E. Farnsworth
Prairie View, Illinois

Notes

1. William James, *The Varieties of Religious Experience.* New York: The New American Library, 1958. P. 378.

2. Helmut Thielicke, *A Little Exercise for Young Theologians.* Grand Rapids: William B. Eerdmans, 1962. P. 11.

3. Clark Pinnock, "Schaefferism As a World View: A Probing Perspective on *How Should We Then Live?*" *Sojourners,* 1977 (July), 34.

4. Ibid., p. 35.

5. Gary R. Collins, "Popular Christian Psychologies: Some Reflections", *Journal of Psychology and Theology,* 1975, *3,* 127-132.

6. This is an application of an idea generated by Al Dueck, "Interpretations of Christ and Culture: The Church, the World and the Profession", paper read at the Twenty-Third Annual Convention of the Christian Association for Psychological Studies, Santa Barbara, California, June, 1976.

7. Jeremiah 9:23,24.

CHAPTER 1

CONCEPTUAL RELATION

People have been trying for years to unite religion and science into a comprehensive worldview. More particularly, committed Christians have been vitally concerned with bringing together Christianity and science, "faith and learning", or their faith and their field. My concern is with theology and psychology and how I can contribute to the uniting process.

The focus in this book will be on the uniting process. I do not intend, however, to start with the end products, or present-day findings, of theology and psychology and from there develop a systematic blend of all of theology and all of psychology. Rather, I will concentrate on the basic processes involved in obtaining the products and in the blending itself. The emphasis will be on activity rather than achievement,[1] on approach rather than answer, on doing rather than done.

The name that is commonly given to any similar enterprise, regardless of its emphasis, is "integration". According to Webster,[2] to integrate is "to form or blend into a whole: unite". One way to go about the process of uniting psychology and theology is to set them in motion in the same direction, with a common reference, and then simply declare that one begins where the other leaves off. Each maintains its own identity, and they are united in purpose (direction) but not in function (interaction with their common reference). An example is Amboise Paré's famous statement, "I bandage, God heals." In other words, I do my thing and God does His, with the shared purpose of helping the same person, but there is no similarity in the two helping processes.

Another way is by again setting psychology and theology in motion in the same direction with a common reference, and then simply averaging similar psychological and theological statements together. The two disciplines would still be united in purpose and perhaps now in function as well, but each would lose its identity. It would be like the two statisticians who were engaged in a wartime battle, crouched behind a bunker. Upon spotting an enemy soldier in the distance, one of the statisticians jumped to his feet, aimed, and took a shot at him, missing to the right. So the other statistician hurried to his feet and fired, but he missed to the left. Excitedly, they turned to each other and vigorously shook hands, exclaiming, "We got him!" Both shots were taken at the same object in a similar way, but were then averaged or pulled to the middle where neither of them actually hit. Unity of purpose and function, but lost identity.

Between the extremes of changing the findings of neither psychology nor theology and changing the findings of both disciplines, is the common practice of changing the findings of one to fit the findings of the other. For example,

1

the Christian psychologist must first provisionally adopt the various ontologies of the researchers from whose work he [sic] wishes to profit. He [sic] then must sort out how their various interpretive "facts" . . . fit together into his [sic] Christian world view. This would result in a good deal of incoherence unless these "facts" were reconceptualized to be something other than what they were said to be in their original interpretive frameworks. Once one has done this, however, . . . he [sic] has settled for an eclectic approach which does not generate a research program having both scientific integrity and conceptual compatibility with Christian theism.[3]

All three of the above examples demonstrate that however well-intended, the integration process can go astray. Most basically, as the second and third examples point out, each discipline should preserve its own identity, because its findings are invalidated when they are averaged with or reconceptualized to fit those of another discipline. In addition, as the first example demonstrates, two fractions of the truth — figuratively speaking — will add together better if they have a common denominator. In other words, I am suggesting that two research findings can be related to each other more fruitfully if there is some similarity in the two research processes. I believe that similarity or common denominator should be the activity of the Holy Spirit. Ideally, this would mean that the Holy Spirit is active in the inquiry of both psychology and theology into their common reference, God's creation. Of course, in addition to the findings of the inquiries needing to maintain their own identity, the methodologies, while being similar concerning the activity of the Holy Spirit, must also maintain their own identity: psychology remains psychology, and theology remains theology.

Integration, as it relates to psychology and theology, has been variously defined. One of the popular current definitions is that it " . . . assumes there is ultimately only one set (configuration) of concepts, laws, or principles which operates in two disciplines . . . . [G]enuine integration involves the discovery and articulation of the common underlying principles of both psychology and the Scripture [sic] . . . ."[4] While an emphasis on discovery and articulation is good, in my opinion it is not complete. What is needed is the further knowledge that comes from application, or living out in one's life. That is, when certain truths are discovered and articulated, they then must become the basis of commitment for action over time in one's life. This allows for a fuller appreciation of the complexities of the truths and therefore for a more complete integration of them.

Without application, one inevitably ends up with "product integration", or "conceptual integration", or more precisely, *conceptual relation*. Closure is reached by intellectually relating similar concepts, but as I have shown, integration has not fully taken place until it becomes "process integration", or more precisely, *embodied integration*. And because of the more applied and prolonged exposure to the concepts, embodied integration is not only the completion but also the verification of their conceptual relation.

Because conceptual relation is the foundation upon which integration rests, I would like to consider it in detail. Basically, it involves relating psychological and theological products or findings, which are the building blocks of the foundation. Generally, they can be grouped into five categories:[5]

1. psychological and theological descriptions of religious experiences and human experience in general;
2. psychological techniques to apply to problems of living;
3. theological rationales for psychological findings;
4. psychological explanations of theological findings;
5. psychological prescriptions and theological imperatives for everyday living.

To conceptually relate any combination of the five kinds of products, two approaches can be taken: manipulation or correlation. That is, seeing if either the psychological or theological product can be subsumed by the other or recast in the other's terms, or if they agree or are at least complementary. Upon reviewing the literature, I have come up with three manipulation models, the Credibility, Conformability, and Convertibility Models. A word of caution: with these three models it is easy to fall into the error of theological or psychological imperialism, whereby one discipline totally subverts the other, changing the actual meaning intended by the subverted discipline's procedures for interpreting its data, and causing the discipline to lose its identity as a discipline. I have also come up with two correlation models, the Compatibility and Complementarity Models.

Models

Credibility Model

The Credibility Model recognizes psychological findings by subsuming them under theological findings. Psychological concepts are seen as secular concepts, which "must be screened through the filter of Scripture" to give them credibility. The guiding principle is that if the teaching of Scripture conflicts with any psychological idea of any kind, the latter will not be accepted as truth, regardless of its empirical support. Lawrence Crabb is a particularly but not uncommonly strong advocate of this position.[6]

Using the Bible as a filter means that the role of theological inquiry in interpreting the words of the Bible is not seriously considered. The cause of such a mentality is two basic misunderstandings. First, it is assumed that *Scripture equals theology*, forcing integrative efforts to focus on the holy data of Scripture and the human discipline of psychology. This data/discipline confusion illustrates the second misunderstanding, that *Scripture complements psychology*. Object-of-studying/process-of-studying categories are mixed, and we have Scripture — the object of studying by theology (the process of studying) — regarded as coextensive to psychology — the process

3

of studying People (the object of studying)! It should be obvious that integration is best served by relating process with process: apples and apples, not apples and oranges.

More accurately, this model gives one human discipline, theology, functional control over another human discipline, psychology, which is okay if the psychological findings are not distorted and psychology as a discipline retains its identity, and if a Christian psychologist merely wants to enhance his or her credibility with the Christian subculture s/he wants to serve.

Conformability Model

The Conformability Model reinterprets psychological findings or reconstructs the discipline of psychology from the perspective of theological findings. This can be called the worldview approach. It means that psychological inquiry and/or its conclusions are filtered through a general Christian perspective or detailed set of "control beliefs". It means that

> . . . we locate each field of inquiry within a Christian understanding of life as a whole, and that we interpret what we know in that larger context. The key ingredients of such a world-view will include the Biblical conceptions of nature, of man, and of history . . . . [T] hese concepts unify our thinking about everything else . . . . All our science and our art, all our social and academic tasks have to do directly or indirectly with nature, man, and history. These concepts, therefore, define the contours of a world-view within which our particular callings take their place. [7]

It means that our set of control beliefs, or worldview, is entirely theologically derived.

Worldview is thought of dichotomously: every discipline has one, and it is either Christian or non-Christian. This is a common presupposition among Christian psychologists and is the necessary condition for one discipline to be carried out in the view of another. Considering another common presupposition, however, that all truth is God's truth, I should think there is ultimately only one worldview as such, and that it is imperfectly approximated by truths from all of the disciplines taken together. Further, if the key ingredients of the worldview are the concepts of nature, man, and history, then all of the disciplines within the natural sciences, social sciences, and humanities can be helpful in defining the worldview.

One's Christian worldview, then, can be seen as the composite, articulated impression of being in the world as a feeling, thinking person that accumulates from inquiry into God's continuous revelation of truth throughout all of His creation. This is much different from a more narrow revelation through just one discipline, which would over time encourage a confusion of the erroneous portion of *tradition* that is inevitably generated when one discipline functions in isolation from others, with God's *revelation*. The limited scope of an isolated theological worldview would obviously be detrimental to fruitful conceptual relation.

4

The worldview approach has two basic variations. One is to reinterpret psychological findings by reanalyzing or even just restating them so they will pass through the narrow theological filter. The literature is full of the resulting Christian perspectives on a wide variety of psychological topics and concepts, an excellent example being the work of Vernon Grounds.[8] The problem is that the data which produced the original conclusions might not be checked to see if they were generated properly. If they are only meaningless artifacts, then any perspective — Christian or not — on conclusions based on such data is irrelevant at best. And, of course, there is always the possibility that the psychological findings might be distorted into something the studies that generated them did not really say.

The other variation of the worldview approach is to use the theological worldview to reconstruct the entire discipline of psychology — the *methodology* as well as the conclusions — the process as well as the products. The worldview becomes a guide for the ethical conduct of psychological inquiry and for the acceptance of psychological findings. It serves mainly as a central core around which acceptable psychological findings fit to help complete the overall picture of God's truth.[9] This certainly affirms psychology as a discipline rather than "keeping it in its place" as the Credibility Model does, but all that is being accomplished is a monitoring of the methods of psychology and the applications of its findings and a legitimizing of certain traditionally-derived psychological findings — only a surface reconstruction of psychology. In addition, as with the reinterpretation variation, psychology remains essentially under the functional control of theology.

An improvement would be to limit the functional control of theology to the usual initial assumption that all truth from the various disciplines is God's truth, but then also that all of creation, including all of the disciplines, is under God's continuous providence. This would, if appropriated fully, incorporate the actual presence of God, through the activity of the Holy Spirit — not just theologically-derived ethical standards — into the methodology of the psychological study. It can be done, I propose, while maintaining the integrity of psychology as a discipline, even though psychological findings would not — in fact could not — continue to be predominantly traditionally-derived.

A second improvement would be to add the resulting psychological findings to the accumulating body of truth or Christian worldview: the composite nature-person-history framework articulated by the ongoing inquiry of all of the various disciplines into God's continuous revealing of truth throughout all of His creation. The two improvements would give psychological inquiry a Person for a Guide, rather than paper for a guide, and would identify worldview more with the product than with the process of the inquiry. The outcome of the universal, unremitting, and unrestricted *activity of God*, rather than a predetermined theological worldview, as the guide for doing psychology and applying its results, would be a more basic reconstruction of the discipline of psychology and a more fruitful conceptual relation of the results of psychological and theological research.

Convertibility Model

The Convertibility Model restricts theological findings to the perspective of psychological findings. This model is most popular among those psychologists who wish to utilize psychological insights to examine psychological aspects and disentangle them from theological aspects of personal religious experiences. The goal is to remove theological cloaks-for-ignorance. [10]

That is fine, but the Convertibility Model is also popular among those religiously-oriented non-Christian psychologists who wish to reduce the credibility of the Bible to a mythical value only. Rollo May gives us an example:

If we . . . look at the myth of Adam as the writers of Genesis presented it, we find . . . [it] portraying the birth of human consciousness . . . . Under the "benevolent dictatorship" of God, Adam and Eve exist in the Garden of Eden in a state of naive, prehuman happiness . . . . But what do they gain as they bid goodbye to Eden? They gain differentiation of themselves as persons, the beginnings of identity, the possibility of passion and human creativity. And in place of the naive, nonresponsible dependencies of infancy, there is now the possibility of loving *by choice*, relating to one's fellowmen because one wants to, and hence with responsibility. The myth of Adam is, as Hegel put it, a "fall upward." It is, indeed, the emergence of human consciousness. [11]

It is obvious that, contrary to the Credibility Model, this model can easily give psychology functional control over theology. May's rendering of "the myth of Adam" as "a fall upward" is a clear case of doing violence to the discipline of theology through psychological imperialism, mentioned above.

Compatibility Model

The Compatibility Model relates psychological findings and theological findings where they agree. Psychologists and theologians who adopt this non-manipulative model give psychological and theological statements equal footing from start to finish (the Compatibility Model is the only conceptual relation model to do so), in order to closely examine and reveal their basic similarities. Thomas Oden provides an excellent example with his parallel listing and analysis of quotations from leaders of the early pietistic movement and the modern encounter culture. [12]

This is useful, in itself or in combination with another model, but it can easily be misused. For instance, one way would be to take a bunch of psychological findings and a bunch of theological findings and just figuratively throw them all into a bucket of water, then let them float around, without examination, to see what sticks to what. Or, simply line psychological findings up on one side and theological findings on the other, where they seem on the surface to be saying the same thing, point for point, and zip 'em up!

A more calculated misuse of the model would be for me to go to the bookshelf and bring down a book containing a very loving statement by the eminent psychologist Carl Rogers: "I hypothesize that growth and change are more likely to occur the more that the counselor . . . prizes his client, as a person, . . . regardless of his particular behavior at the moment."[13] As I develop Rogers' thought, I realize that Jesus also spoke to the theme. So I race through nine different translations until I discover just the right words: "But now I tell you: love your enemies, and pray for those who mistreat you."[14] The misuse is to then assume that a synthesis of the two produces an idea that is truer than either idea alone. If something is true in the first place, it cannot become truer!

Complementarity Model

The Complementarity Model relegates psychological and theological findings to different levels of description — each tells a different story. In Malcolm Jeeves' use of this model,[15] the assumption is made that psychology provides "spectator" accounts of reality as opposed to the "actor" accounts of theology. Further, since actor accounts deal with the who and why of reality, they are of a higher order than spectator accounts that deal with the what and how of reality. Therefore, since theology describes the Who as well as the who and the why, and psychology describes the what and the how, they have a hierarchical relationship with theology at a higher level.

In this model, theological findings are usually assumed to presuppose psychological findings, giving them perspective and revealing their significance in fresh categories, subordinating but not altering them, in contrast to the Conformability Model. In contrast to the Compatibility Model, theological and psychological findings are related, but not by matching them up side-by-side and word-for-word, as in Figure 1, where the first three findings do not match but the fourth findings do. Rather, the relation is shown by including a specific psychological finding under a perhaps more general theological finding that gives it a broader perspective, as in Figure 1, where specific psychological finding number "1" is included under general theological finding letter "A".

Whereas technically the Complementarity Model can place either discipline atop the hierarchy, in its usual form this position is occupied by theology. This is only natural, because of the assumption that psychology's orientation is completely spectator/experimental. Such a view, however, unnecessarily excludes the equally viable participation/humanistic orientation that describes the who and why of personally lived human reality. This reorientation of psychology, which does not challenge the theological position regarding the more ultimate questions of the Who and why, will be discussed in Chapter Three.

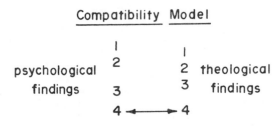

Compatibility Model

psychological findings — 1 2 3 4 ⟷ 4 — 2 3 theological findings

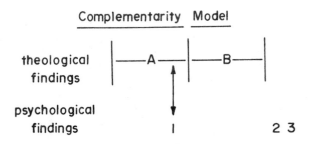

Complementarity Model

theological findings | ——A—— | ——B—— |

psychological findings   1   2 3

Figure I.

The guiding principle of the model is threefold. First, psychology and theology have a common reference — a created, ordered universe continuously upheld by God. Second, each is in principle exhaustive within its own methodological limitations. That is, both psychology and theology can ultimately achieve their own purposes without need for each other — although neither is sufficient alone for the larger purpose of describing reality as a whole. Their findings are related, but their methodologies are independent. Third, although the two types of findings are related, they make entirely different assertions — this is the defining characteristic of the Complementarity Model.

As a brief summary critique of the five conceptual relation models, I prefer the modified Conformability Model and the two correlation models for providing a foundation for embodied integration. The Complementarity Model has the advantage of potentially bringing more psychological and theological findings into relation than does any other conceptual relation model. The modified Conformability Model has the advantage of being the only model that incorporates the activity of the Holy Spirit — the proposed common denominator for research processes whose results are to be conceptually related — into the conduct of psychological inquiry. And all three models substantially provide for the basic requirement that psychology preserve its identity as psychology and theology preserve its identity as theology.

Notes

1. "Integration should be seen not as an achievement or a position but as an intellectual activity . . . " — Arthur F. Holmes, *The Idea of a Christian College.* Grand Rapids: William B. Eerdmans, 1975. P. 48.

2. *Webster's New Collegiate Dictionary.* Springfield, Massachusetts: G. & C. Merriam, 1977.

3. David L. Wolfe, "Reflections on Christian Empiricism: Thoughts on William Sanderson's Proposal", *Christian Scholar's Review,* 1978, *8,* 45. Note: I have highlighted the sexist language here but not in later quotes, in the interest of readability.

4. John D. Carter, "Secular and Sacred Models of Psychology and Religion", *Journal of Psychology and Theology,* 1977, *5,* 202, 205. Relating "principles of both psychology and the Scripture", it should be noted, is a mixing of categories — see my discussion of the Credibility Model.

5. The first three were brought to my attention by Clinton W. McLemore, "The Nature of Psychotherapy: Varieties of Conceptual Integration", paper read at the Twenty-Third Convention of the Christian Association for Psychological Studies, Santa Barbara, California, June, 1976.

6. Lawrence J. Crabb, Jr., *Effective Biblical Counseling.* Grand Rapids: Zondervan, 1977.

7. Arthur F. Holmes, *All Truth Is God's Truth.* Grand Rapids: William B. Eerdmans. 1977. Pp. 125, 128.

8. Vernon Grounds, *Emotional Problems and the Gospel.* Grand Rapids: Zondervan, 1976.

9. See Gary R. Collins, *The Rebuilding of Psychology: An Integration of Psychology and Christianity.* Wheaton, Illinois: Tyndale House, 1977.

10. See William Sargant, *Battle for the Mind: A Physiology of Conversion and Brain-Washing.* London: William Heinemann, 1957.

11. Rollo May, *Psychology and the Human Dilemma.* Princeton: D. Van Nostrand, 1967. P. 219.

12. Thomas C. Oden, *The Intensive Group Experience: The New Pietism.* Philadelphia: Westminster, 1972.

13. Carl R. Rogers and Barry Stevens, *Person to Person: The Problem of Being Human.* Lafayette, California: Real People, 1967. P. 94.

14. *Good News for Modern Man.* New York: American Bible Society, 1966. Matthew 5: 44.

15. Malcolm A. Jeeves, *Psychology & Christianity: The View Both Ways.* Downers Grove, Illinois: Inter-Varsity, 1976.

CHAPTER II

EMBODIED INTEGRATION

When I think about the manna story in Exodus 16, I cannot help but think of embodied integration. Here is a story of continuous struggle between trusting in human provision and trusting in God's provision. The nation of Israel, having come out of Egypt, into the wilderness, has not yet arrived in Canaan. It seems to me that this is precisely our own present-day struggle as individuals: through our trust in God and obedience to His provision in Jesus Christ, we have been delivered out of the slavery of total reliance on human provision, into the wilderness of learning how to faithfully rely on God's provision through obedience to His will.

It is a very difficult psychological/spiritual journey that we are on. What it takes to complete the journey, for us (having gotten out of totally human provision, getting into God's total provision) as for the Israelites of old (having gotten out of Egypt, getting into Canaan), is the same trusting obedience to God that led to our initial deliverance. And that is a tremendous psychological/spiritual struggle. Regardless of how seemingly inconsequential something may be, the comfort and security that it temporarily provides subtly creep into and increasingly take a powerful grip on our redeemed but not fully emancipated lives. The idolatry of looking, for example, to shopping as one's principal source of enjoyment, to walking around a shopping mall as a release from boredom, and/or to buying something new to break through one's depression, is indeed hard to be liberated from.

The psychological power of consumerism reaches deeply not only into our personal lives but also into our relationships with others. By continuing to surround oneself with possessions and to accumulate wealth and varying types and increasing amounts of insurance as a protection for the future, one no longer needs to engage in sharing relationships with others. With survival so heavily assured, who needs others? Who needs *koinonia*? Who needs the church?

As a Christian who is a psychologist, it is appropriate for me to present psychological and theological descriptions of the effects of consumerism and psychological and theological suggestions regarding lifestyle to liberate people from those effects. These descriptions and suggestions pertaining to consumerism can be conceptually related to each other in a variety of ways (see the models in Chapter One), but the process cannot stop there. What is needed is the further knowledge that comes from application. Does it work? Does God really provide? Can I give testimony only intellectually about God's provision, or can I tell about how God has been concretely providing and will continue to provide in my life? Only the wilderness experience of actually living out the truths that have intellectually delivered me can teach me the complete truth of the matter. That is what I call embodied integration.

Regardless of the example, consumerism or whatever, it should be pretty obvious that wherever the integration of two disciplines is concerned, the bottom line is always the activity of God. Since God is the Author of all creation, everything that might come under investigation by any particular discipline is thereby part of God's creation and therefore being continuously upheld by Him.[1] The purpose of integration, then, is fully knowing God's truths in His creation, or in other words, knowing God. It follows that each inquiry, be it psychological or theological, is actually living with God. It is by living with God that the psychologist and the theologian know God and His truths.

The opening up of both disciplines to be integrated to the activity of the Holy Spirit, by defining them as particular ways of living with God so as to know His truths, incorporates the Holy Spirit's involvement in several ways. It is important to note that not only is this the direct involvement of upholding the objects of study and indirect involvement in the monitoring of the methods of psychology and theology and the applications of their findings, but most significantly the Holy Spirit is also necessarily included in the generating of the data. However, whereas the Holy Spirit has generally been assumed to take at least a partial guiding role in all aspects of theological inquiry, such has definitely not been the case with psychological inquiry. What is needed is the basic reconstruction of psychology referred to in Chapter One in the discussion of improvements of one of the variations of the Comformability Model. As a step in that direction, toward a Spirit-filled psychology, I have outlined what a reconstructed psychology might entail in Chapter Three.

Humanness

Having stated that the purpose of integration is knowing God, and having defined both psychology and theology as particular ways of living with God, I cannot emphasize enough the importance of relationship and communication with God in the process of generating data. It is equally important to emphasize that in order to communicate with God, whether we are doing research or not, we must have contact with Him. And contact is based on similarity: the similarity we have with God is our humanness, or our person/ spirit dimension.

> In other words, for man to receive spirit, man must be spirit himself. If man is to receive sense impressions, he must be sensual; if he is to assimilate food, he must be organic in nature; if he is to receive images and ideas and hold them, he must be intellectual; if he is to be held responsible to certain prescriptive laws, he must be volitional. Likewise, if God is to come as Holy Spirit and dwell with man, man must be spirit to be truly "present" with God . . . . This can only mean, in modern terms, that God is *Person*, and man is *person*, and that they are truly and fully "present" with each other only on the level of interpersonal relationship.[2]

Knowing God and living with God are based on communication with Him, is based on contact with Him, is based on similarity with Him, is based on *our humanness*.

Humanness, however, is precisely the self-reflective, personally responding dimension of existence that is controlled out of present-day psychological research and that has traditionally been ignored in theological studies. That will be an important focus of the following two chapters, and the synonymous usage of "person" and "spirit" will be dealt with in Chapter Five.

It should be obvious that our humanness is an integral part of the entire integration process. From the generating of the data that lead to the products that are conceptually related, to the living out in one's life of those truths, humanness is a key factor. We might put it another way and say that humanness is an important aspect of the entire truthing process. Integration is, after all, a process of knowing God's truths. So by saying that humanness is crucial to the integration process, I am thereby saying that it is crucial in knowing God's truths.

Knowing truth and integrating are not only both vitally affected by humanness, they are essentially the same thing. Therefore, a full description of how we go about knowing God's truths should give us a complete picture of the integration process. For the remainder of this chapter, then, I will discuss knowing truth.

Knowing Truth

I prefer not to supply a "quick and dirty" definition of truth, for example truth is that which conforms to reality, because such definitions are usually circular. In this case, one would ask what the definition of reality is and get the answer that reality is that which is true. Rather, I prefer to discuss how truth is appropriated or taken into one's life. This does not deny the importance of sophisticated analysis in the production of truth claims, but rather puts such analyses into proper perspective. Analysis, then, in and of itself does not "prove" a statement to be true but brings the statement to my attention as something I should take seriously — seriously enough to not only *believe* that it is true but also to *act* as though it is true. The reality is less that I should demand proof from truth and more that truth demands a response from me! If I then incorporate the truth claim into the way I live, I still have not "proven" it, but I have done the best I can to qualify for advertising it as truth.

My conclusion is that truth exists in spite of me but that it does me no good unless I appropriate it. That is when it becomes truly objective, when I am involved enough with it to know its "object" qualities, or its beneath-the-surface complexities. If I get too far away, saying that I know *objective truth* without any attempt to make it true for me, I run the risk of it becoming *projective truth*, or what I imagine it must be. So, the aspect of knowing truth that I will emphasize is using what reasonably seems to be true as a framework for interpreting personal experience and as a guide for making responsible choices.[3]

Parameters for Knowing Truth

I prefer also to be straightforward about ways we are limited in knowing truth. This can especially be seen in the initial, analysis phase of knowing truth, and can be described as parameters or boundary conditions. Following are five such limitations:

Knowing truth in Scripture. It should be obvious that every person who reads Scripture brings to that interpretive task, for better or worse, who s/he is as a person. This includes biases from cultural conditioning and personal pathologies as well as Christian maturity. The latter is a factor when we bring to our reading of Scripture what God has shown us through previous experiences, including other readings of Scripture. Without this bringing of past learning to a new learning situation, maturity would be meaningless. Since our personhood can thus serve to help us to discover deeper truths, or in other cases to hinder us from discovering any truth at all, knowing truth in Scripture is not a matter of immaculate perception![4]

Knowing all the truth in Scripture. I believe that God speaks in Scripture for all time, but that I will never, in all of my Twentieth-Century exuberance, fully grasp everything God has to say in His propositional revelation. I think this is why Scripture is appropriate for every age and why people must continue to read and reread it frequently. Scripture does not change, but people do . . . .

Knowing truth in other ways. I believe that God does not traffic only in ideas, or words. In addition to His propositional revelation (Scripture), He communicates nonverbally through existential revelation (religious experiences such as prayer and general psychological experience such as feelings) and natural revelation (human and nonhuman physiology and behavior). Religious and psychological experiences are ways of communicating with and knowing God, not merely knowing about God. They entail "hearing" God in ways other than through written words — "conversing" with the Holy Spirit without reading Scripture. To investigate them, one must move beyond the restrictions of the natural science method, which reveals the more general and less personal truths that God has created an ordered universe and has given a natural order for the living of our lives.

Knowing truth through various disciplines. Since God reveals His truths in a variety of ways, various disciplines other than theology are needed to interpret revelations other than Scripture. Further, since all academic disciplines are subject to human error, no one discipline should be made subservient to any other.[5] This is why the preservation of the identity of disciplines is so basic in the generation and conceptual relation of their products. An example of how this works out in the articulation of biblical truths is the authen-

14

tic challenge provided by natural scientific findings to a theological conclusion of a literal seven-day creation. Another is the authentic challenge provided by psychological evidence to theologically-derived sex-role stereotyping.

Knowing all of God's truth. As finite beings, we should not presume to know all that God knows nor even all that He has for us to know through His propositional, existential, and natural revelations. The created is by definition less than the Creator, so we are by nature characterized by what we might call "human epistemic finitude." The Apostle Paul said it well: "At present we are men looking at puzzling reflections in a mirror. The time will come when we shall see reality whole and face to face! At present all I know is a little fraction of the truth, but the time will come when I shall know it as fully as God has known me!"[6] Several Old Testament references also forcefully make the point: Deuteronomy 29:29 — the secret things belong to God, but the revealed things belong to us; Ecclesiastes 8:16,17 — even though we seek laboriously to discover everything there is to know, we cannot succeed; Isaiah 55:8,9 — God's thoughts are not our thoughts.

Types of Truth

Within the five parameters for knowing truth, several types of truth can now be presented that are involved in and describe the entire integration process. The idea of types of truth, I might interject, is contrary to the belief of those psychologists and theologians who claim to possess all of the truth in a general sense. The only category of truth we could describe for them would be "exclusive truth". It is also contrary to those radical experimentally-oriented psychologists who believe "truth" is merely a mechanical structure that precludes choice, and to those radical humanistically-oriented psychologists for whom "truth" is merely the act of choosing!

Exhaustive Truth. This type of truth results from technical inquiry into (1) nature, God's natural revelation, and (2) the Bible, God's propositional revelation. Put another way, it results from a detached, third-person perspective rather than an involved, first-person perspective. It is "exhaustive" in that it results from natural scientific and "scientific" theological methodologies that leave no gap within the ultimate limits of what they can achieve. ("Scientific theology" will be the primary focus of Chapter Four.) Natural science and scientifically-oriented theology can approach the end of what their methodologies can accomplish without any apparent need for completion or verification of their methods by another, "nonscientific" discipline. They stand on their own two feet.

I prefer not to use the term "Propositional Truth" as the truth category for those truths provided by the Bible, as Francis Schaeffer does.[7] I think "Exhaustive Truth" more adequately represents how truth is arrived at through the process of preliminary discovery (reading) of scriptural proposals

15

d hypotheses that become, through careful articulation (exegesis), axiotic postulates and predictions. The only way I could stand outside of th and personally proclaim it as such, by saying the Bible *as it sits there* itains "propositional truths", would be if I were God. In other words, I st first bring the Bible "in here" by reading it — but a first, cursory ding yields only possibilities, perhaps nothing very solid. It is only after I down to the hard work of studying and analyzing what I read that it jins to take on the weight of axiomatic postulation and prediction.

Deriential Truth. This type of truth results from personal inquiry into the momenal worlds of people. A person's phenomenal world is his/her sonal arena for God's existential revelation through individualized perceptions, feelings, and meanings. This is the realm of humanistically-oriented chological and theological inquiries into human experiences and religious periences, respectively.

Historically, there has been a strong tendency to investigate only the onal or irrational aspects of religious experiences. "We can have a valid iceptual knowledge of God....But... there is another knowledge of d which goes beyond concepts, which passes through concepts to attain n in the mysterious actuality of His presence, grasped in some sort, in an perience.' "[8] This experience beyond concepts is referred to by Rudolf o as a third category, the nonrational and intuitive that needs no reflection — a "creature-feeling" — a "unique original feeling-response" — indeed, "primal bottom". And, according to Otto, " ... it can be firmly grasped, roughly understood, and profoundly appreciated, purely in, with, and n the feeling itself."[9]

wo points of clarification might be helpful at this point. First, whereas edrich Schleiermacher was the first to view religious experience in this /, he mistakenly saw consciousness of God as resulting from inference, or *coning to a cause outside of oneself for an inner feeling concerning self.* Contrariwise, Otto sees consciousness of God as resulting from *eptivity, or responding to an objective reference outside of oneself with eling concerning the outside object,* not merely the inner self.

Second, whereas the rational is an essential part of religious experience is not the whole of it, the surplus of meaning which is the nonrational is the entirety of the experience either. Using Otto's favorite simile, both e to be investigated together as the warp and the woof of the complete ic. The proper course for theological inquiry into religious experience, n, is a gradual completion — rationalization, moralization, and humanization — of the nonrational by progressively charging it with rational, moral, cultural significance. This is a process

..whereby [the nonrational] passes ... into the region of the conceivable and omprehensible. Yet all the time all the elements of non-rational "inconceivability" re retained ... and intensified as the revelation proceeds. "Revelation" does not iean a *mere* passing over into the intelligible and comprehensible. Something may be profoundly and intimately known in feeling for the bliss it brings or the agitation it produces, and yet the understanding may find no concept for it. To *know* and to *understand conceptually* are two different things . . . . And so, too, St. Paul "knows" the peace which yet "passeth understanding".[10]

Contingent Truth. This type of truth results from corroboration of Exhaustive Truth or commitment to Experiential Truth. Scientific and biblical facts cannot be absolutely proven, so they are contingent upon repetitious study to eliminate plausible rival hypotheses and reach consensus. We cannot know phenomenological facts with absolute certainty either, so we commit ourselves to the authority of that which we say is true and begin to live out its implications for our lives. Contingent Truths are what are conceptually related, utilizing one of the models from Chapter One. In other words, after discerning that the results of corroboration of an Exhaustive Truth and commitment to an Experiential Truth seem to be saying the same thing, the next task is to relate them so they are "in fact" saying the same thing. That may involve a little manipulation or just straight correlation, with the hoped-for result in either case of a deeper conception of the truth of the matter. Caution: not truer, but deeper.

A distinction needs to be made here between being "absolutely" certain and being certain. *Being "absolutely" certain* leads to dogmatism ("I'm right"), which creates vanity (believing that *I* have the *truth*), all of which most likely emanates from fear. *Being certain*, on the other hand, generates enthusiasm ("I've bet my life"), which creates humility (believing that the *truth* has *me*), all of which emanates from faith. I don't just buy a Bible and carry it around in my hand, advertising "I have the truth." But I do say, with exultation, "I belong to Jesus!" I appropriate Jesus Christ as my personal Lord and Savior, and at that moment the Truth has me!

"The truth has me" — that is a beautiful concept. That great Dane, Sören Kierkegaard, expressed it vividly: "The truth is a snare: you cannot have it, without being caught. You cannot have the truth in such a way that you catch it, but only in such a way that it catches you."[11] And the way that it catches you is through your commitment. It is similar to buying a dog. I have the dog not when I initially purchase him, but after I feed him, play with him, and begin to train him. Then he has me, just as much as I have him.

Commitment to the Exhaustive Truths of experimental psychology and "scientific" theology and/or the Experiential Truths of humanistic psychology and theology that I say are true, as a framework for interpreting my experience and as a guide for making responsible choices, consistently in all areas of my life, is the process over time of Contingent Truths becoming *truths for me.* That completes the circle: the truth has me and is truth for me. It also crosses the line: knowing God "out there" becomes knowing God "in here"; conceptual relation becomes embodied integration.

Some people would say at this point that the embodied integration of Contingent Truths is appropriate because "All truth is God's truth." This is a very popular expression but a bit misleading. I think it most accurately refers to God's revelation, which is the source of all truth and is all God's. Truth is there — it is revealed — but we have to discover it. And since we cannot absolutely prove that the Exhaustive and Experiential Truths that we discover, articulate, and embody are in fact God's truths as opposed to not really truths at all, I think we ought to leave it as a prior assumption — all truth is God's truth — and not use it as a concluding summary — all the truths we found are God's truths.

Comprehensive Truth. This final type of truth is approached as truths for me begin to systematically comprise the entire disciplines of psychology and theology. And as truths for me from other disciplines are included, until all of the inquiries into God's truth that seem sufficient for my way of knowing and capacity for knowing are represented, an overall "worldview" begins to take shape (as discussed in Chapter One). Worldview is another name for Comprehensive Truth. How this develops is shown in Figure 2, which is a summarizing picture of the entire integration process.

Figure 2 assumes excellence at the *beginning point* in the psychological and theological inquiries into God's truth. It assumes that the person who wants to integrate the two disciplines either does good psychology and good theology or demands good psychology and theology from those psychologists and theologians whose products s/he conceptually relates and then commits him/herself to as truth. What constitutes good psychology and good theology will be the subject of later chapters. But this is a tremendously important point, because the whole integration effort will be tainted if we simply accept psychology and theology as they are, as given systems, thereby limiting the discovery/articulation process to available psychological instruments and safe theological categories.

A paraphrase of one of Johann Goethe's more memorable remarks is that if you treat things like they are, you make them worse; if you treat them like they can and should be, you make them better. Consider the following:

> Scientific investigation in psychology has always been tied more to philosophical assumptions about the nature of man and the nature of science . . . than many have recognized. If erroneous and overly simplistic assumptions about the nature of man are made at the outset, and the researchers are unfortunate enough to obtain the predicted results for the wrong reasons, then a massive waste of research effort can result . . . . Since the results appeared to support these popular notions, they were uncritically accepted into the body of psychological knowledge. Once such "knowledge" gets into the field, it becomes a difficult but necessary task for those later working out a new and different framework to remove it by explaining it from that new perspective. [12]

And,

> the printed Word tells you half the story, and your heart's experience the other half . . . . [So,] the world, the Church and women are suffering sadly from woman's lack of ability to read the Word of God in its original languages. There are truths

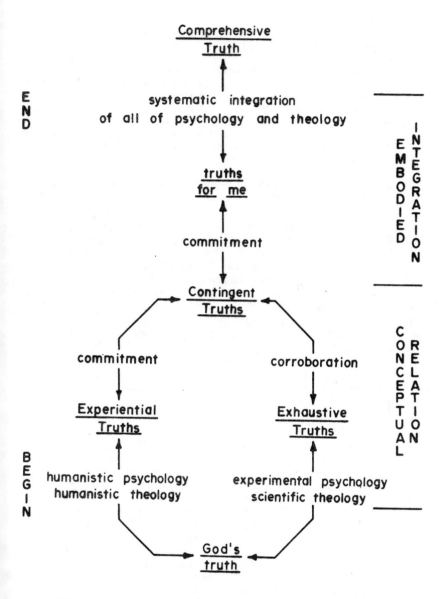

Figure 2.

therein that speak to the deepest needs of a woman's heart, and that give light upon problems that women alone are called upon to solve. Without knowledge of the original, on the part of a sufficient number of women to influence the translation of the Bible in accordance with their perception of the meaning of these truths, these needed passages will remain uninterpreted or misinterpreted . . . . We must remember that no translation can rise much above the character of the translator . . . .He cannot properly render what has not as yet entered in the least into his own consciousness as the truth . . . . "Men only need . . . to bring to the Bible sufficiently strong prepossessions, sufficiently fixed opinions, to have them reflected back in all the glamour of infallible authority" . . . . Supposing *women only* had translated the Bible, from age to age, is there a likelihood that men would have rested content with the outcome?[13]

Obviously, both psychology and theology must be treated as they should be, not as they are. But if they are appropriate at the beginning point, then the integration process can proceed up either side or both sides concurrently in Figure 2. That is, experimental psychological findings and scientific theological findings can become Contingent Truths through the basic scientific procedure of publicly verifiable replication, and then become embodied through commitment to them as truths for me. Likewise, humanistic psychological findings and humanistic theological findings can become Contingent Truths through an initial commitment to their rather limited authority in my life, and then become embodied through commitment to them over time, in all areas of my life, as truths for me. I must remember, however, that in either case the result is not as comprehensive as when both sides of the diagram are involved.

The *ending point* in Figure 2 is not necessarily a comprehensive, systematic integration of all of psychology and theology. This is because living out truths in our lives takes time and effort. The essence of integration, embodied integration, is commitment to truths, not simply comparison of truths, as is the case with conceptual relation. As we verify the psychological and theological truths we have conceptually related, by committing ourselves to them over time, we will be transformed, a process that may take a very long time. So we must wait on the Lord, not rush into premature expression of what we only think is true. If I "wait for the Lord", as the psalmist says,[14] He will call me in His own time to express what He is showing me in a loving way that will bring honor and glory to Him and further His kingdom. My expression may not be a book or a series of sermons. It may just be a single idea. But if that idea totally permeates my life, then it will indeed be a powerful testimony of knowing God's truths by living with God.

Think of the implications for church services, among other things, where members of the body would share embodied truths-for-them rather than delegate the responsibility to one person to sermonize truths-for-everyone. Truth for me can be truth for everyone if it is God's truth, but I cannot know everything everyone else needs to know. Nor can a singer sing every song everyone might want to hear. In deciding what to record for a new album, s/he can choose either hit songs or songs from his/her life. Likewise, in deciding what to write about in a new book, I can choose topics from pop psychology and/or pop theology, or I can choose *songs from my life.*

In conclusion, I would like to dramatize the difference between conceptual relation and embodied integration. To me, the differences are very similar to those between desegregation and integration (desegregation is naming an all-white Catholic church in an all-black neighborhood Our Lady of the Courageous Caucasions!). Seriously, John Cartwright makes the following comparisons: [15]

1. desegregation "is mere association"; integration "is community";

2. desegregation "is neighborhood"; integration "is neighborliness";

3. desegregation "at best . . . will only create a society where men and women are physically desegregated and spiritually segregated, where elbows are together, but hearts are apart; it gives us social togetherness, and spiritual apartness; it leaves us with stagnant equality of sameness, rather than a constructive equality of oneness."

Conceptual relation, when not completed by the embodiment stage of integration, leaves us with mere association rather than with community, with mere comparison rather than with commitment. Psychology and theology are left *elbows together, but hearts apart.*

Notes

1. Biblical documentation would proceed something like this:
"By faith we understand that the worlds were prepared by the word of God, so that what is seen was not made out of things which are visible" (Hebrews 11:3), "in the beginning was the Word, and the Word was with God, and the Word was God. He was in the beginning with God. All things came into being through Him; and apart from Him nothing came into being that has come into being" (John 1:1-3), and "God, after He spoke long ago to the fathers in the prophets in many portions and in many ways, in these last days has spoken to us in His Son, whom He appointed heir of all things, through whom also He made the world. And He is the radiance of His glory and the exact representation of His nature, and upholds all things by the word of His power" (Hebrews 1:1-3a); so " . . . He is before all things, and in Him all things hold together" (Colossians 1:17); " . . . there is but one God, the Father, from whom are all things, and we exist for Him; and one Lord, Jesus Christ, through whom are all things, and we exist through Him" (I Corinthians 8:6); *therefore,* "This is the day which the Lord has made; Let us rejoice and be glad in it" (Psalm 118:24) — *New American Standard Bible.* Philadelphia: A.J. Holman, 1973.

2. Arnold B. Come, *Human Spirit and Holy Spirit.* Philadelphia: Westminster, 1959. P. 73.

3. Walter R. Thorson, "The Concept of Truth in the Natural Sciences", *Themelios,* 1968, *5* (2), 27-39. See also Walter R. Thorson, "The Spiritual Dimensions of Science". In C.F.H. Henry (Ed.), *Horizons of Science: Christian Scholars Speak Out.* New York: Harper and Row, 1978.

4. See Berkeley Mickelsen and Alvera Mickelsen, "Does Male Dominance Tarnish Our Translations?" *Christianity Today,* 1979 (October 5), 23-29.

5. A fine example of the mutual contribution of two disciplines to each other, in this case philosophy and theology, is Arthur F. Holmes, *Philosophy: A Christian Perspective: An Introductory Essay.* Downers Grove, Illinois: Inter-Varsity, 1975.

6. J. B. Phillips (Trans.), *The New Testament in Modern English.* New York: Macmillan, 1972. I Corinthians 13:12.

7. He also uses Exhaustive Truth and Experiential Truth as categories, but defines them differently than I am defining them here. See Francis A. Schaeffer, *Genesis in Space and Time.* Downers Grove, Illinois: Inter-Varsity, 1972.

8. Thomas Merton, *No Man Is An Island.* Garden City, New York: Doubleday, 1967. P. 173.

9. Rudolf Otto, *The Idea of the Holy: An Inquiry into the Non-Rational Factor in the Idea of the Divine and Its Relation to the Rational,* trans. John W. Harvey, 2nd ed. New York: Oxford University, 1950. P. 34.

10. Ibid., p. 135. Paul may not have been able to adequately put it into words, but he *knew* the love of Christ (Ephesians 3:19) and the peace of God (Philippians 4:7).

11. Ronald Gregor Smith (Ed.), *The Last Years: Journals 1853-1855 by Sören Kierkegaard,* trans. Ronald Gregor Smith. New York: Harper & Row, 1965. P. 133.

12. Monte M. Page, "Demand Characteristics and the Verbal Operant Conditioning Experiment", *Journal of Personality and Social Psychology,* 1972, *23,* 376, 377.

13. Katherine C. Bushnell, *God's Word to Women.* North Collins, New York: Ray B. Munson, 1923 (reprint). Paragraphs 12, 13, 375, 154, 372. See also Rollo May, *Love and Will.* New York: Norton, 1969. Pp. 236, 237. What cannot be conceived cannot be perceived: "For the act of perceiving also requires the capacity to bring to birth something in one's self; if one cannot, or for some reason is not yet ready, to bring to birth in himself some position, some *stance* toward what he is seeing, he cannot perceive it."

14. Psalm 27:14.

15. From an address given for Black Emphasis Week, Trinity College, Deerfield, Illinois, February, 1977.

CHAPTER III

A PSYCHOLOGICAL BASIS FOR INTEGRATION

He takes the saints to pieces,
   And labels all the parts,
He tabulates the secrets
   Of loyal loving hearts.
He probes their selfless passion
   And shows exactly why
The martyr goes out singing,
   To suffer and to die.
The beatific vision
   That brings them to their knees
He smilingly reduces
   To infant phantasies.
The Freudian unconscious
   Quite easily explains
The splendour of their sorrows,
   The pageant of their pains.
The manifold temptations,
   Wherewith the flesh can vex
The saintly soul, are samples
   Of Oedipus complex.
The subtle sex perversion,
   His eagle glance can tell,
That makes their joyous heaven
   The horror of their hell.
His reasoning is perfect,
   His proofs as plain as paint,
He has but one small weakness,
   He cannot make a saint. [1]

The modern psychologist too often manages to accomplish just what the poem says: s/he takes people to pieces, smilingly reducing their beatific visions, the splendour of their sorrows, and the pageant of their pains to proofs as plain as paint. That's the complaint leveled at psychologists by Rollo May:

You have spent your life making molehills out of mountains.... When man was tragic, you made him trivial . . . ; and when he drummed up enough courage to act, you called it stimulus and response. Man had passion; and when you were pompous and lecturing to your class you called it "the satisfaction of basic needs," and when you were relaxed and looking at your secretary you called it "release of tension." You made man over into the image of your childhood Erector Set or Sunday School maxims . . . .

In short, [you were sent] to a Dantean circus, and you spent your days and nights at sideshows![2]

One of the main reasons for the trivializing of visions and sorrows, courage and passion, etc. is that psychological research tends to exclude first-person accounts of lived experience. For example, hypotheses are formulated, experiments designed, and statistical data collected, but hardly ever is collaborative dialogue between those who are subjects and those who are experimenters a part of the process. Hardly ever is the subject asked to provide in his or her own way a personal account of his or her reactions during an experiment, much less a detailed personal account of the pageant of a psychological process such as pain.

The exclusion of first-person accounts of lived experience, of course, means the exclusion of the self-reflective, personally responding dimension of existence called humanness. But the cost is potentially very great, because as discussed in Chapter Two, humanness is crucial in knowing God's truths. When humanness is ignored, then the activity of the Holy Spirit in the conduct of psychological inquiry is extremely limited. Yet in the great majority of psychological investigations conducted by Christians, this is precisely what happens. Whereas God may be assumed to be upholding what is being investigated, and perhaps may even be included in part of the overall investigation by the psychologist prayerfully monitoring the methods and applying the conclusions, He is not expected to be part of the actual generating of the data leading to those conclusions. God's activity is apparently no more than a detached upholding of only two facets of His creation — the object of psychological study and the ethical conduct of the study and application of its results. But He most assuredly is not purposefully expected to actively uphold a third facet of His creation, the studying itself.

In fact, humanness, and thereby much of the activity of the Holy Spirit, are actually designed out of the standard psychological experiment. "If psychologists aim to predict and control human behavior and experience, as in their textbooks they claim, they are assigning man to the same ontological status as weather, stars, minerals, or lower forms of animal life . . . . Scientific psychology has actually sought means of artificially reducing variance — humanness — among men, so that they will be more manipulable."[3] Humanness is controlled out of the participants in "well-designed" experimental psychological inquiry by the deliberate assignment of personal feelings, meanings, and values to "contaminating variables", "error variance", and "residual matrices". B. F. Skinner regards such basic human expressions as "epiphenomena", "mental way stations", and "explanatory fictions".[4] This makes the experimenter detached rather than involved and the subject a passive respondent rather than an active participant.

The effect is to deny the personal participation in the experiment of both the subject and the experimenter, resulting in both being dehumanized. This amounts to one nonperson studying another nonperson! It leaves us with what C. S. Lewis referred to as "men without chests".[5]

The problem is graphically portrayed in Figure 3.[6] Notice that psychology must be included in the "natural world" column of Figure 3, where psychology's source of data — persons — must reside as part of God's general revelation ("the Bible" column being His special revelation). This is appropriate for experimental psychology, which has traditionally been construed as a "social science" employing natural science methods.

Notice also in Figure 3 that guidance by the Holy Spirit is limited to "the Bible" column. This simply highlights the fact that the activity of the Holy Spirit is not at all expected to be part of natural scientific methodology, and therefore of the methods of psychology.

Psychology in general is concerned primarily with understanding how people go about living their lives. For nonexperimental or humanistic psychology, however, that includes some of the items from the right-hand side of Figure 3, such as meaning, purpose, why questions, and I-thou relationships. Also, the primary concerns on the left-hand side are with control rather than service and with objects rather than persons. Yet part of humanistic psychology's concern with understanding people is very much related to viewing them as persons and not as objects and to helping them to live better lives. For these reasons, I am very uncomfortable with the entire discipline of psychology being relegated to the left-hand side of the figure.

I believe that the nonperson paradigm, whereby humanness is controlled out of psychological research, does not adequately represent the discipline of psychology. Psychology as a *natural science* is appropriate for some research goals, but not for all. "[The scientist] has to recognize . . . that there are many aspects of reality which can be known only through becoming involved with them, so that in order to have knowledge of these he is obliged, by his own ruling principle of 'openness to evidence', to give up scientific detachment."[7] Therefore, to appropriately place psychology into Figure 3, we need a column down the middle. We need to develop psychology as a *human science.*[8]

I want to emphasize that I do not believe that psychology as a human science should now become the new paradigm for the entire discipline of psychology. Nor do I believe that none of God's truths can be discovered using natural science methods for understanding people as people.

God does indeed work in mysterious ways, and perhaps one of those ways is through the "intuition" of the experimenter:

Conventionally the investigator has operationally defined concepts such as stress, incentive, frustration, and so forth in terms of some manipulable experimental condition and then gone on to study the consequent behavior in order to make inferences about the basic psychological processes under investigation. In other words, instead of determining from the subject how he perceived the situation in order to interpret his behavior, the investigator has decided for the subject what the situation was supposed to mean, and, assuming that he was correct in his interpretation, has drawn inferences from the behavior. In many instances this procedure works because, intuitively putting himself in the subject's place, the investigator correctly surmises how the subject

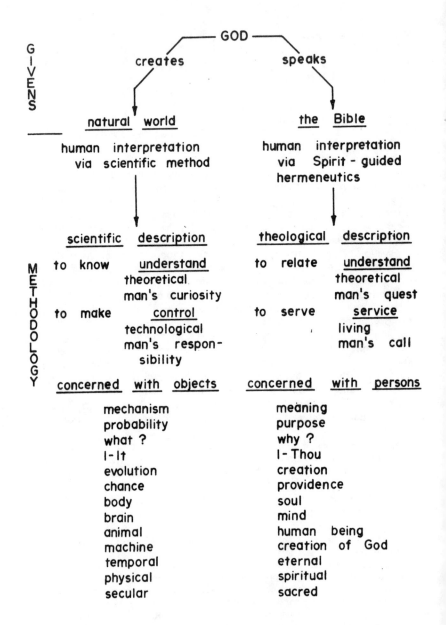

Figure 3.

26

perceives the situation. We might say that this experimental model has functioned because the investigator has unwittingly taken advantage of information about what may have been going on in the subject's experience . . . ."[9]

Could not this information have come from God? The purpose of psychology as a human science would be to make any such communication from God more by design than by "accident".

Conduct of Inquiry

How can we design the activity of the Holy Spirit *into* the conduct of psychological inquiry, so that it will enhance the integration process? How can we involve the Holy Spirit in a more significant way than in just the upholding of the created, ordered universe and of the intellectual honesty and personal integrity of the investigator in analyzing the data and applying the conclusions (through the middle, not just at the two ends of the investigation)? In answering these questions, I will look at three aspects of the conduct of psychological inquiry: mentality; motive; method.

Mentality

Since the integration process depends upon an adequate methodological beginning point (see Chapter Two), any reconstruction of psychology that offers an alternative to the limitation of available methods dictating the questions that are asked, should be a good thing. The alternative I am proposing — a Spirit-filled psychology — however, is vulnerable to contamination from a variety of mentalities, which also have negative effects on integration.

The dogmatizer. A person with this mentality has a fear that to have an open mind is to have an empty one. So s/he tends to inadvertently close down the working of the Spirit before fruitful conceptual relation can take place. S/he becomes, for example, prematurely and unreasonably certain that theological findings are truer than psychological findings (I call this "hardening of the categories"). Perhaps this reduction of two different truths relating to each other on potentially equal terms to one truth being automatically in hierarchical relationship to the other is because of a strong need for order and simplicity. Or perhaps s/he simply is intolerant of the ambiguity of not knowing for sure or with "absolute certainty".

The folly of premature closure is that " . . . we live [from womb to tomb,] bottle-to-basket on a learner's permit. The tragedy is that much of what we learn is a false certainty pasted over the deeper ambiguities of existence."[10] One danger is that it reinforces the self-perpetuating belief that "safe" theological categories are unquestionably true because everybody in one's subculture says so. Another danger is that it negatively feeds the already

27

dogmatic mentality of the Credibility Model, making it inappropriate for integration.

The dichotomizer. This person ultimately forces things into polarities. Accordingly, the dichotomizer would tend to arrive at a conclusion like this: "God made the world, and God gave the Bible. Men make Science and men make theology." [11] This obviously pulls the Holy Spirit and people apart! With models that tend to polarize anyway, such as the Conformability Model and the Complementarity Model, the dichotomizer mentality could certainly make integration inappropriate.

Religiofication. This mentality is the turning of practical purposes into holy causes, [12] or giving psychological concepts divine sanction. It is reifying a psychological construct and then deifying the reification (a sneaky move of those psychologists I call "Ph. Deities")! It is also "rearranging the revelation":

> [The Church] conciliates and collaborates with the world, accepting every compromise in the hope of salvaging a little something. She is only too happy when, thanks to her successive theological disavowals, she can say, "Look! At last there are some Marxist intellectuals, or some workers, who have been willing to listen to what we have to say." That is the perpetual justification of collaborators. There is Freudianism, which cannot be rejected because it is science. So we have to rearrange the revelation in order to come up with something which will fit in with it. [13]

Imagine trying to formulate and conceptually relate psychological and theological findings, with a religiofication mentality and utilizing the Convertibility Model! I am afraid the Holy Spirit would get pushed around a bit.

The synthesizer. This person believes that a combination of two ideas is truer than either idea alone. This sets the stage for a manipulative use of both psychology and theology, whereby each loses its identity and is used for other purposes. An example of a sythesizer is Aaron going along with the Israelites rebelling against the one, invisible God. He decided to have gods (plural), beginning with a golden bull (visible), and then tried to baptize the new ideas and direct them toward the Lord. Aaron tried to combine the best features of the various religions, and in the process each lost its identity. Contrast Aaron with Jesus, the full representation of God and man; the Word made flesh; the perfect integration.

The synthesizer mentality would severely hamper the conceptual relation of psychology as psychology and theology as theology, especially if it were linked up with a model such as the Compatibility Model, as pointed out in Chapter One. Imagine saying that what Carl Rogers says, if true, plus what Jesus Christ says is truer than what either one says alone!

The legitimizer. A person with this mentality is just and conciliatory toward the handling of any attitudinal differences regarding the relative status of psychological and theological truths. The legitimizer is similar to the synthesizer, in that both regard two truths as legitimate and allow them to intermingle on potentially equal terms to produce a fruitful combination. They differ, however, in that the synthesizer changes both truths in the process so they are unrecognizable in the final combination, or at least are considered to be less true than the final combination. The legitimizer, on the other hand, changes or devalues neither truth itself, so the combination of them will retain the original identity of each (what it is and where it came from) and not be considered to be truer than either of them, alone.

The legitimizer differs more obviously from the other three mentalities in being more open-minded, more accepting of phenomena without fear or favor. "The genuine will to know calls for the spirit of generosity rather than for that of economy, for reverence rather than for subjugation, for the lens rather than for the hammer."[14] Subjugation is in varying degrees an attribute of the three manipulation conceptual relation models, and economy is often an attribute of the two correlation conceptual relation models. Generosity and reverence are the attributes of Spirit-filled psychological inquiry, of the legitimizer mentality that accompanies it, and of the model that fruitfully conceptually relates its findings.

Motive

There are also many motives that can complicate the bringing of the Holy Spirit actively into the inquiry and thoroughly into the integration process. A common type of motive that is often associated with psychology and theology is represented by the secular/sacred conflict. That is, a person who is doing psychology and trying to integrate psychological and theological findings can easily be motivated by a desire to demonstrate the superiority of the secular (psychology) or the sacred (theology) or simply to demonstrate their similarity. Following, I will briefly list Niebuhr's well-known classification of the conflict,[15] along with possible effects on psychological inquiry and conceptual relation that each could have as a motive.

Christ against culture. To resolve the conflict between the secular and the sacred, one must choose either Christ or culture, thus maintaining the antagonism. With a model with a dogmatic mentality, such as the Credibility Model, this motive would be devastating for both psychology and integration.

Christ above culture. In Christ, human aspirations reached their highest culmination, but He also brought in Himself something that neither arose out of culture then nor contributes very directly to it now. With this as a motive, one is not against culture, just above it all. Also with this as a motive, the impotency-by-definition of the Holy Spirit would make it not a very Spirit-filled psychology, and the polarization of the unmodified Conformability Model would make integration even more counterproductive than without the biasing effects of such a motive.

Christ of culture. Christ was simply the highest fulfillment of cultural aspirations. He was a most highly developed man, but not God. If utilized as a motive as a part of the Convertibility Model, integration of *evangelical* theology with *Spirit-filled* psychology would certainly not be possible.

Christ and culture. One accommodates the other. One implication is to obey society's institutionalized forms of knowledge — mainline psychology and theology — and hope for ultimate justification. That is to say, with a motive of what is is right, [16] we hope that some psychological or theological finding that we have accepted as given and zipped up all nice and tidy is not later "disproven", leaving our Compatibility Model unzipped and us exposed. This, of course, could happen with any "truth" that is being conceptually related or even embodied. The point is that with this easy-going, accept-it-as-it-is attitude, skills will not be developed to critically analyze the new, conceptually related truth claim in terms of what constitutes good psychology or theology. It will be embraced in place of the old just because it is new.

Opposed to this conforming, rather faddish approach is a willingness to challenge the professional orthodoxy and an ability to evaluate the adequacy of the methodologies that gave rise to the old and new truth claims, before accepting one over the other. Or perhaps it would lead to illuminating the old in the light of the new. Perhaps it would be discovered that the same truth has been grasped all along but not in as enriched a way. What makes such an enriched view possible is not just reciting what "psychologists tell us", but knowing what constitutes excellence, in this case, in psychological inquiry.

Passive acceptance of the status quo could also negatively affect the Complementarity Model, by furthering its deficiency in the mutual interrogation of the two disciplines being related. There would be an awfully passive acceptance of the Holy Spirit in the psychological inquiry, too, I am afraid.

Christ transforming culture. This is the resolution of the secular/sacred conflict that proclaims a historic Christ fulfilling, transcending, and actively intervening in culture. [17] This motive, along with a mentality of generosity and reverence, would be most appropriate for the Spirit-filled psychological inquiry and embodied integration process that I am proposing. With an open-minded search for God's truths, revealed by a God who is actively intervening in the arena of psychological inquiry, one is well-prepared for considering a method for the conduct of the inquiry.

Method

The question is, now, how can we design the activity of the Holy Spirit into the methodology of psychological inquiry? First, we must look at what it is that a Spirit-filled psychology studies.

Levels of inquiry. I have found it helpful to employ a levels of inquiry model that relates psychology to other ways of knowing and the areas of life that need to be known.

> Science is *not* regarded as complementary to the Bible. The created natural world is regarded as complementary to the revealed world of the Bible . . . . If we recognize that we have trustworthy revelation from God both in the natural world and in the Bible, can we not then cease from pursuing these false dichotomies: science or Scripture, evolution or creation, natural or God-caused . . . ?[18]

This translates, with the addition of "phenomenal worlds" to represent the everyday worlds of human experience through which God also reveals Himself as part of general revelation, into:

$$\frac{\text{humanities} - \text{science}}{\text{Bible} - \text{phenomenal worlds} - \text{nature}},$$

where there are two levels of inquiry. One is the level of the knowing processes (inquiry), and the other is the level of what needs to be known (revelation).[19] Humanistic theology and psychology as a human science are included in "humanities", whereas scientific theology and psychology as a natural science are included in "science".

A person's everyday

> . . . *world* and *nature* are not the same thing. By world we are referring to what everyone knows naively and is directly experienced by all men; nature, in contrast, is the world viewed under a very special attitude — one that strips all objects of their relationship to living beings — and thus nature comes to mean physical and inert matter . . . . "Worlds", on the other hand, are correlates of consciousness that know them as such, and in order to understand worlds, one must follow their implications back to the human subjects. Nature, too, is the correlate of a conscious attitude, but its meaning is such that the reference back to the conscious structure that knows it is not pursued. Nature is to be treated only in its relationships to other material or spatio-temporal things, but not in the way this network of relationships is supported by a special structure of consciousness. Thus, in this conception of science, the difference between the domain of "nature" and that of "world" is such that one cannot extend the concepts, procedures, and findings from one to the other without serious distortion.[20]

Psychology as a human science, then, studies phenomenal worlds; psychology as a natural science ideally studies only nature. Psychology studies the Bible only indirectly, by revealing inadequacies in theological statements and peculiarities In the personalities of theologians who make such statements. The latter is called "psychotheology".[21] Figure 4 summarizes what primarily studies what.

God reveals His truths to psychological study ideally via two clearly distinct routes, natural science and human science. These two routes can also be called experimental and phenomenological, as shown in Figure 5.[22]

INQUIRY		REVELATION		
scientific theology	special	Bible	written words	propositional
humanistic theology		phenomenal worlds	religious experiences	existential
human science psychology	general		general psychological experience	
natural science psychology		nature	human and nonhuman physiology and behavior	natural

Figure 4.

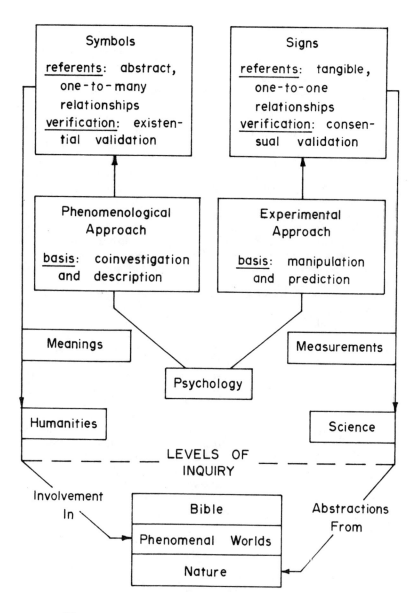

Figure 5.

Several terms on the left-hand side of Figure 5 indicate what a Spirit-filled psychology might entail. Terms such as "phenomenological", "coinvestigation", "existential validation", and "meanings" offer the possibility that all participants in psychological research can be open to the working of the Holy Spirit for the revealing of God's truths through their humanness. What do the terms mean?

Phenomenological. This term refers to two things: an attitude; an approach. It is an attitude of appreciation of God's propositional, existential, and natural revelations as they present themselves, and of respect for personal experiencing of God's ongoing revelation. It is an approach rather than an answer to existence, through careful description of lived experience — what is personally meant rather than what is impersonally measured.

Methodologically, a phenomenological approach is based on an alternative to manipulation (or deception) and prediction, which are the basis for much of psychology today. Because of this alternate basis for research, phenomenological approaches communicate and build trust rather than mistrust. This offers a tremendous opportunity for the Holy Spirit to work through people to communicate His truths.

Figure 5 summarizes the phenomenological approach in general: a coinvestigation for the existential validation of the personal meanings in one's phenomenal world.

Coinvestigation. This is a methodological emphasis on asking and doing for and with (dialoguing), rather than telling and doing to (manipulating). It is, in my opinion, the most effective psychological framework for the discovery of Experiential Truths, discussed in the previous chapter. It is based on the two fundamental notions that (1) the knower personally participates in the knowing process,[23] and (2) in the process of knowing, we are in-formed by the thing understood while simultaneously we give form to the thing we understand.[24] That is, the investigator is never a totally detached spectator but is always involved with the object of observation to some degree, and the process of observation is always one of reciprocity. Coinvestigation also brings the coinvestigator (otherwise known as the "subject") into the investigation as s/he really is, as an active participant rather than a passive respondent, thereby getting at experience as it is personally lived rather than impersonally predicted.

Phenomenological coinvestigation answers questions like those posed by Argyris:[25]

Is it possible to create a psychological set on the part of the subject so that he is involved in giving as accurate replies as he can *and* in keeping the researcher informed as to when he (subject) is becoming defensive or could become defensive? Can the subject be helped to become as objective and verbal as he can about his subjectivity? Under what conditions can subjects be motivated to be so involved in the research that they strive to give valid data and warn the researcher when they (or others) may not be giving valid data?

34

Further,

> we can begin to change the status of the subject from that of an anonymous *object* of our study to that of a *person*, a *collaborator* in our enterprise. We can let him tell the story of his experience in our studies in a variety of idioms. We can let him show what our stimuli have meant to him through his manipulations of our gadgetry, through his responses to questionnaires, with drawings, and with words. We can invite him to reveal his being. We can prepare ourselves so that he will want to produce a multi-faceted record of his experiencing in our laboratories. We can show him how we have recorded his responses and tell him what we think they mean. We can ask him to examine and then authenticate or revise our recorded version of the meaning of his experience for him. We can let him cross-examine us to get to know and trust us, to find out what we are up to, and to decide whether he wishes to take part. Heaven knows what we might find.[26]

God knows what we *will* find!

Existential validation. This process is essentially commitment to the authority of an Experiential Truth and beginning to live out its implications in one's life, thereby making it a Contingent Truth. But the personal transformation that results from such commitment is only half of the existential validation process. The other half is communication.

In a phenomenological inquiry, two coinvestigators have not existentially validated what an experience symbolizes to one or the other of them, or how it is true for him or her, until that meaning is similarly understood by them both.[27] R. D. Laing portrays very clearly just how difficult it is for two people to understand each other.[28] His thesis is that the only way to understand another person is through experience — my behavior does not directly affect your behavior; behavior is to experience as figure is to ground or a word is to its context. Figure 6 is a picture of what Laing calls "interexperience".[29] I do something; I behave in some way; I tell you something that has a particular meaning for me. You experience my behavior by perceiving and interpreting it in view of the demand characteristics (whatever situational cues you experience as suggesting or compelling a certain kind of response) of the situation we are in, whatever expectation(s) you might have brought along with you, and whatever you might be fantasizing about at the moment. You in turn behave back to me (speak, smile, etc.) in a way that represents for you your experience of my behavior. I in turn experience your behavior in terms of my perception and interpretation(s). So far, on the surface, I may have simply said, "I'm a Christian," and you may merely have replied, "Oh . . . ." But it is obvious there is much more to it than the behavior itself.

As I in turn behave a second time and start the ellipse once again, it gets even more complex but closer to good communication. And as we continue on through several ellipses, we begin to dialogue, we more clearly understand each other, and we existentially validate my initial behavior and its meaning for me.

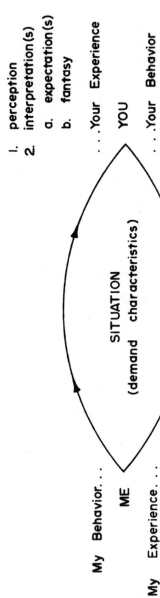
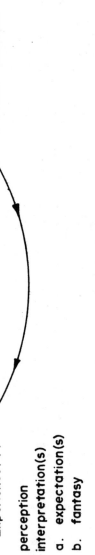

My Behavior...
ME

1. perception
2. interpretation(s)
   a. expectation(s)
   b. fantasy
My Experience...

SITUATION
(demand characteristics)

1. perception
2. interpretation(s)
   a. expectation(s)
   b. fantasy
...Your Experience
YOU
...Your Behavior

Figure 6.

36

Meanings. The fourth reference term from Figure 5 refers to the basic data of a Spirit-filled phenomenological psychology.

> Neither behavior nor experience are [sic] ever fully and exhaustively captured. It would be impossible to do so. However, the fact that behavior and experience are different cannot be ignored either, so that the manner in which these two aspects of man become data for psychology must also differ. Behavior becomes data when its relevant aspects are measured, and experience becomes data when subjects meaningfully describe the relevant aspects of the . . . situation. Perhaps it can be briefly summarized by saying that meaning is to experience what measurement is to behavior.[30]

It is very important for our purpose of doing Spirit-filled psychology that we appreciate the concrete differences between experience and behavior. The most direct way I can say it is that rather than behavior being "outside" and experience "inside" the person, it is, depending on one's perspective, exactly the reverse![31] From my view, your behavior is certainly outside and your experience inside of you. But at the same time, my behavior is inside and my experience outside to me. That is, I cannot see my behavior, but what I do "see" is my experience. My *experience* is what is obvious to me, whereas I need feedback from you as to how I am behaving or coming across. You need to tell me what I am nonverbally communicating, that I am not consciously aware of, that makes me appear to be giving double messages (contradicting what I say with how I say it). Only through an unfolding interexperience dialogue, then, can I fully get in touch with what I mean and accurately communicate that meaning to you. It seems to me that only in this way can I hope to be an open channel through which the Holy Spirit can communicate truth so that it will be heard.

Another "internal" and very important aspect of meaning is *intentionality*. Intentionality " . . . gives meaning to experience . . . . Each act of consciousness tends *toward* something, is a turning of the person toward something, and has within it, no matter how latent, some push toward a direction for action."[32] Intentionality is this situating/orienting and incorporating/drawing into consciousness that " . . . is not to be identified with intentions, but is the dimension which underlies them; it is man's capacity to have intentions."[33]

Further, " . . . our meanings are never purely 'intellectual' . . . . Intentionality . . . goes below levels of immediate awareness, and includes spontaneous, bodily elements and other dimensions which are usually called 'unconscious'."[34] Thus, I am already bodily preconceptually involved in situations before having words for it. Intentionality is walking somewhere but nowhere in particular; saying something I didn't "mean" to; "unconsciously" stepping on a bee while standing in place giving a lecture on ecology; being prayerful without uttering words.

By including this aspect of humanness in the conduct of psychological inquiry, we are incorporating the active involvement of the Holy Spirit in a most significant and valid way. For even when the Word of God strikes a man without warning, when there is a sudden conversion, an inner call, which changes all at once the direction of his life, he perceives that God has been speaking to him for a long time, that the dialogue was already going on in the darkness of the unconscious before it broke out into the full light of day.[35]

The tragedy is that when the only method we have does not allow us to ask the right questions, the experience as it is actually lived is never known. And the activity of the Holy Spirit is not accurately known. Nor is God's truth....

Notes

1. G. A. Studdert Kennedy, "The Psychologist". Cited in W. E. Sangster, *The Path to Perfection*. New York: Abingdon-Cokesbury, 1943.

2. Rollo May, *Psychology and the Human Dilemma*. Princeton, New Jersey: D. Van Nostrand, 1967. P. 4.

3. Sidney M. Jourard, *Disclosing Man to Himself*. Princeton, New Jersey: D. Van Nostrand, 1968. Pp. 4, 6.

4. Skinner employs this terminology in his chapter and comments in T. W. Wann (Ed.), *Behaviorism and Phenomenology: Contrasting Bases for Modern Psychology*. Chicago: University of Chicago, 1964.

5. C. S. Lewis, *The Abolition of Man*. New York: Macmillan, 1947.

6. Taken, with slight modification, from Richard H. Bube, "Notes on 'Science and the Whole Person' — A Personal Integration of Scientific and Biblical Perspectives, Part 3: The Philosophy and Practice of Science", *Journal of the American Scientific Affiliation*, 1976, *28*, 129.

7. Donald M. MacKay, *The Clock Work Image: A Christian Perspective on Science*. Downers Grove, Illinois: Inter-Varsity, 1974. P. 38.

8. For an in-depth development of this statement, I recommend Amedeo Giorgi, *Psychology as a Human Science: A Phenomenologically Based Approach*. New York: Harper & Row, 1970. Also, from a Christian standpoint, C. Stephen Evans, *Preserving the Person: A Look at the Human Sciences*. Downers Grove, Illinois: Inter-Varsity, 1977.

9. Martin T. Orne, "Hypnosis, Motivation, and the Ecological Validity of the Psychological Experiment". In W. J. Arnold & M. M. Page (Eds.), *Nebraska Symposium on Motivation, 1970*. Lincoln: University of Nebraska, 1971. P. 232.

10. T. George Harris, "Jung & Old", *Psychology Today*, 1971 (Dec.), 43.

11. Richard H. Bube, "Towards a Christian View of Science", *Journal of the American Scientific Affiliation*, 1971, *23*, 3.

12. Eric Hoffer, *The True Believer: Thoughts on the Nature of Mass Movements*. New York: Harper & Row, 1951.

13. Jacques Ellul, *Hope in Time of Abandonment*, trans. C. Edward Hopkin. New York: Seabury, 1973. P. 133.

14. Herbert Spiegelberg, *The Phenomenological Movement: A Historical Introduction* (Vol. 2), (2nd ed.). The Hague, Netherlands: Martinus Nijhoff, 1969. P. 657.

15. H. Richard Niebuhr, *Christ and Culture*. New York: Harper & Row, 1951.

16. Jacques Ellul, *The Technological Society,* trans. John Wilkinson. New York: Alfred A. Knopf, 1964.

17. What I am really talking about here is a redirection of Niebuhr's apparent assumption that the primary culture-transforming activity of Christ is directly in or toward the entire culture (many people believe the "Christ transforming culture" position accomplishes this the best). In contrast, I see that as only a secondary transformation. Christ's intervention is probably most powerful through Christian *sub*cultures, created alongside and within the structures and institutions of the world to *indirectly* further the kingdom of God in the larger culture (I call this "alternative subcultural witnessing"). All Christian and nonChristian institutions, because of the fallen spiritual beings called powers and principalities that influence if not control them, participate in the fallen human condition. They must therefore be reformed, replaced, or redeemed. But the question is, how? "Should I continue to try to bring about change in this institution (or profession) through *personal* Christian witness, or should I just leave?" "If I choose an alternative, *communal* Christian witness (or an alternative psychology), do I have to be antagonistic toward and live totally separate from the culture (or psychology) I am reacting against (the "Christ against culture" position)? Or, must I be accommodating and just accept any tensions that may arise between the two options (the "Christ and culture" position)?"

The position I am suggesting is living *alternatives* and as *allies*: (a) participating, in obedience to God in a loving way that will bring honor and glory to Him and further His kingdom, in an alternative subcultural group — a covenanting community — oriented around alternative lifestyles, celebrations, technologies, occupations, and/or institutions (or an alternative psychology), alongside or within but always in *mutually beneficial dialogue* with the institutions of the secular and Christian worlds (or with mainline psychology) — this is neither antagonism nor accommodation, but advocacy; (b) allying with the oppressed, the poor, the needy, and with other subcultural witnessing groups in promoting justice (or with others who are developing psychology as a human science) — in other words, taking on others' burdens, living among the oppressed as an equal, rather than dispensing just enough charity from afar to maintain a superior status (or doing psychological research within a trust relationship of "coinvestigators" rather than with "subjects", who are kept in an inferior status through deception and manipulation).

My position is summarized well by Clark Pinnock, "An Evangelical Theology of Human Liberation, Part 2", *Sojourners,* 1976 (March), 27-29. "Recognizing the reality of fallen powers makes us cautious about [the] 'Christ the transformer of culture' model in connection with our social concerns . . . . Some Christians suppose that social change will come about when individuals are converted and have their attitudes changed . . . . Others . . . advocate . . . that we ought to seek to gain power and use it Christianly. While there is truth in both these proposals, the Bible points us to a third strategy which sees change coming about through the presence in history of the people of God, a 'city set on a hill,' a microcosm of what human life can be under the rule of God. This community serves to present outsiders, including the powers themselves, with a preview of the new age . . . . [It] . . . exists not to serve itself but to bless the world by mediating Christ's servanthood in the midst." John Howard Yoder's "The Paradigm of Peoplehood", *Inside,* 1974 (January-February), 28-31, is an excellent amplification of Pinnock's statement. The most systematic and concise foundational support for both is Hendrik Berkhof, *Christ and the Powers,* trans. John H. Yoder. Scottdale, Pennsylvania: Herald, 1962.

18. Bube, "Towards a Christian View of Science", pp. 3, 4.

19. This is the distinction made in Chapter One between discipline and data, or the process of studying and the object of studying.

20. Amedeo Giorgi, "Phenomenology and the Foundations of Psychology". In J. K. Cole & W. J. Arnold (Eds.), *Nebraska Symposium on Motivation, 1975.* Lincoln: University of Nebraska, 1976. P. 292.

21. "All theology is psychotheology. The objective is to first study the psychology of a theologian and then to study his theology" — John G. Finch, Ph.D., personal communication, September, 1976; "Should we try to understand a doctrine from its overt content, or from the psychological make-up and the biography of its author? We must seek an understanding from all these angles simultaneously, everything has meaning . . . . All these views are true provided that they are not isolated . . . " — Maurice Merleau-Ponty, "What Is Phenomenology?" trans. Colin Smith. In J. D. Bettis (Ed.), *Phenomenology of Religion: Eight Modern Descriptions of the Essence of Religion.* New York: Harper & Row, 1969. P. 27.

22. Adapted from Joseph R. Royce, "Psychology is Multi-: Methodological, Variate, Epistemic, World View, Systemic, Paradigmatic, Theoretic, and Disciplinary". In J. K. Cole & W. J. Arnold (Eds.), *Nebraska Symposium on Motivation, 1975.* Lincoln: University of Nebraska, 1976. P. 52.

23. Michael Polanyi, *Personal Knowledge: Towards a Post-Critical Philosophy.* New York: Harper & Row, 1964.

24. May, *Love and Will.*

25. Chris Argyris, "Some Unintended Consequences of Rigorous Research", *Psychological Bulletin,* 1968, *70,* 194.

26. Sidney M. Jourard, "Experimenter-Subject Dialogue: A Paradigm for a Humanistic Science of Psychology". In J. F. T. Bugental (Ed.), *Challenges of Humanistic Psychology.* New York: McGraw-Hill, 1967. P. 113.

27. "Your laws say that if two men agree on something that has happened, their witness is accepted as [valid]" — *The Living Bible.* Wheaton, Illinois: Tyndale House, 1971. John 8:17.

28. R. D. Laing, H. Phillipson, and A. R. Lee. *Interpersonal Perception: A Theory and a Method of Research.* New York: Harper & Row, 1966.

29. Ibid., adapted from p. 12.

30. Amedeo Giorgi, "The Experience of the Subject as a Source of Data in a Psychological Experiment". In A. Giorgi, W. F. Fischer, & R. Von Eckartsberg (Eds.), *Duquesne Studies in Phenomenological Psychology: Volume I.* Pittsburgh: Duquesne University, 1971. P. 55.

31. Robert Romanyshyn, "Phenomenology and Behavior: Contributions of Merleau-Ponty", paper read at the Eighty-Third Annual Convention of the American Psychological Association, Chicago, Illinois, September, 1975.

32. May, *Love and Will,* pp. 223, 230.

33. Ibid., pp. 223, 224.

34. Ibid., pp. 229, 234.

35. Paul Tournier, *The Meaning of Persons,* trans. Edwin Hudson. New York: Harper & Row, 1957. P. 162.

CHAPTER IV

A THEOLOGICAL BASIS FOR INTEGRATION

Almighty and everlasting God, lift the curtain of light, the light of day that causes me to look down, that reveals the smallness of my life with You and the dust and pettiness of my life with others.

Give me the darkness that causes me to look up, that reveals the vastness of my life with You and the wonder and mystery of Yourself.

As Jacob of old, help me to hold fast to You in the darkness, where my words fail but Your presence is truly felt.

Help me to not hide You with words, while satisfying myself that I now, somehow, have more of You.

Help me as I search the mystery of Yourself; keep me from thinking that because I have named You, I possess You.

At this moment, in this place of silence, while I invoke the darkness, I give to You, simply, my awe and wonder and worship.

In silence . . . .

Amen[1]

As Jacob held fast to the Angel of God, as if aware that the impending daylight would rob him of his anticipated blessing, so too, perhaps, do we more nearly approach God in darkness than in light. Perhaps we know more of God when we approach Him more in simple awe than with complicated conception. Perhaps, at least at times, God is known more in the vastness of silence than He is through the precision of words.

Therefore, while we need a psychology that does not dehumanize me by reducing me to a machine, *denying* my personhood, we also very much need a theology that does not dehumanize me by reducing me to a mind, *restricting* my personhood. If I were only a mind, then I could know God only while thinking — aloud or to myself, in either case breaking the silence. That would restrict both the activity of the Holy Spirit and my humanness. But just as modern psychology overemphasizes behavior (to the exclusion of experience), it seems to me that modern theology does in fact overemphasize thought (to the exclusion of feelings).

The overemphasis on thought takes place in two ways. One is in viewing the Bible as God's only revelation. The Exhaustive Truths contained in Scripture are seen by many evangelical theologians as the necessary and sufficient means to all truth. The other main area of theological inquiry, which happens to be part of God's existential revelation — religious experiences — is not viewed as a part of revelation as such. Products from only part of the overall field of theological inquiry therefore become "exclusive truths". This negates the need not only for truth from a large portion of the discipline of theology itself, but also from any other discipline, such as psychology.

43

Such a narrow limiting of possibilities for how God can communicate truths, all of which are His, reveals a lack of awareness that *knowing about God* is not the same as *knowing God.* Truly personal knowledge, relationship, and fellowship cannot be fully communicated through verbal propositions alone. Was not the knowledge of good and evil discovered through the eating of the forbidden fruit, rather than by hearing or even reading about it? Was not the Ark of the Covenant Israel's visible but nonverbal sign of God's presence with them?

The other area of overemphasis on thought is in regarding the experience of reading the Bible as a purely, and sometimes even pure, mental act. I noted in Chapter Two that knowing truth in Scripture is *not* a matter of immaculate perception and in Chapter Three that we are always bodily/ preconceptually involved before we are mentally involved in our situations. No situation is purely mental. Nor is it initially mental.

Whereas reading the Bible is not founded on the *purity* of perception (the entire reading process), it is founded on the *primacy* of perception (the initial sensing aspect of the reading process — the more precise use of the term "perception"). That is, prereflective or preconceptual sensing is prior to and the foundation for reflective thought or conceptualization. Perception founds thought.[2] Albert Einstein, one of the greatest reflective thinkers of our time, once described it this way: "The words of the language as they are written or spoken do not seem to play any role in my mechanism of thought. The psychical entities which seem to serve as elements in thought are certain signs and more or less clear images . . . . [T] hese elements are, in my case, of a visual and some of a muscular type. Conventional words or other signs have to be sought for laboriously only in a secondary stage."[3] It becomes obvious that reading the Bible is not the work of a mind but of a mind/body, a person. So, one might say, when reading the Bible, the Holy Spirit is involved before, during, and after words!

I also mentioned in Chapter Two that the Holy Spirit is more active in the doing of theology than in the doing of psychology. We should not, however, let that fact lull us into a false sense of theological security. By restricting humanness in theological inquiry into the written words of Scripture and even the phenomenal worlds of persons (as foreign as religious experience usually is to theological inquiry) to verbal-mental experience only, the work of the Spirit is also restricted. In other words, I am not so sure we have a Spirit-filled theology either.

The wholeness of the person — mind *and* body — will be the emphasis of this chapter. The unbalanced, fragmented view of the person, however, has at least two deleterious effects that will need to be discussed. One such effect is to mire us in the mind-set that theological inquiry is totally a reasoning, non-feeling process. The products of such inquiry become "facts uncontaminated by feelings", without any acknowledgment of the fact that this aspect of humanness is needed in the truthing process. We are thereby encouraged to experience our theological efforts all in our heads, through ideas only, thereby causing our integrative efforts to be top-heavy. Maybe that is why we have been falling flat on our faces!

The other effect is to perpetuate some very loose, often carelessly defined anthropological terminology describing the physical/psychological/spiritual makeup of persons. I believe this in particular to be another pervasive obstruction to integration.

The purpose of this chapter will be to suggest correctives to the restrictions on the involvement of the Holy Spirit in the conduct of theological inquiry and the integrative process that result in part from the first effect of a fragmented view of the person. The second effect will be the central focus of Chapter Five.

Conduct of Inquiry

What correctives to the dehumanizing of persons and restricting of the activity of the Holy Spirit can be made in the conduct of theological inquiry? Can the Holy Spirit be involved in additional ways to the blessing and mental guiding of the reading of Scripture? To answer these questions, I will focus once again on three factors of any inquiry — mentality, motive, and method.

Mentality

Of all the mentalities that can accompany the doing of theology, I think the most damaging is "platonic thinking".

Platonic thinking. This is forcing what we perceive into dichotomies, in much the same way as the dichotomizer mentality described in Chapter Three. Perhaps the most pervasive manifestation of this mentality is the split between the material and the spiritual, the secular and the sacred, the body and the soul.

"The resurrection and ascension prove there is no reason to make a false dichotomy between the spiritual and the material. That is a totally nonbiblical concept."[4] Had God wanted us to know of a totally "spiritual" resurrection, He would have raised Christ as a formless, bodyless spirit. But Christ appeared, ate food, and was touched! It is clear to me that Scripture does not get caught up in Plato's immortality of the soul, but speaks of the resurrection and ascension of the body, the totality, the *Gestalt.*

Another, probably even more damaging version of platonic thinking is the division of people into rational (the accuracy of reason), as good, and irrational (the untrustworthiness of feelings), as bad. I believe this simply reflects our rebellion against God and our own created nature.[5]

Emil Brunner, in a chapter titled "Biblical Psychology", describes the schism between "the chill of reason" and "the warmth of feeling", which causes reason to become impersonal and feeling to become the focus of the irrational. To restore both of these important aspects of our created nature, as well as the balance between them, he emphasizes the need for a proper view of feeling.[6] Toward that end, Viktor Frankl states, "Feeling can be much more sensitive than reason can ever be sensible."[7]

Furthering the argument, Rollo May asserts that feelings are not just a chance state of the moment nor a push from the past (the reason why), but a pointing toward the future (the purpose for).[8] And to create a balance between feeling and reason, he declares (substituting "feeling" for "wish" and "reason" for "will") that "[Feeling] gives the warmth, the content, the imagination, the child's play, the freshness, and the richness to [reason]. [Reason] gives the self-direction, the maturity, to [feeling]. [Reason] protects[feeling], permits it to continue without running risks which are too great. But without [feeling], [reason] loses its life-blood, its viability, and tends to expire in self-contradiction."[9]

I think one of the finest examples of the fact that feelings are worthwhile and used of God is Abraham Heschel's point that hardness of heart may be from God. He argues that hardness of heart is cured when it is made absolute (half-callousness seeks no cure). When hardness of heart is complete, it becomes despair, and out of despair prayer bursts forth. "Prophets came and went; words had no effect, turbulent punishments, miseries, were of no avail . . . . Where signs and words from without fail, despair within may succeed . . . . The weird miracle of callousness, resistance to God, may be due to an obstinacy imposed by God."[10]

"O Lord, why have you hardened our hearts and made us sin and turn against you? Return and help us, for we who belong to you need you so."[11] What a beautiful statement of restoration and renewal of relationship. If that is what it takes to get me on my knees, to finally look to God for my strength and to rejoice in the sufficiency of my relationship with Him, then praise the Lord.

Whole person. As a corrective to the platonic thinking mentality, I propose a whole-person mentality. I believe the involvement of the Holy Spirit will be far greater if theological inquiry will refrain from dichotomizing the material and the spiritual, the sensible and the sensitive. By working with our entire created nature, our undiminished humanness, I believe we will be working more completely with God, both in the studying of the Bible and by taking the analysis of religious experience much more seriously.

The Bible always shows man as a unity, and always, in his totality, "in his place before God." The terms σῶμα (body), σάρξ (flesh), ψυχή (soul or mind), νοῦς (mind), do not in the Bible refer to distinct parts of man, attached together in some way, but "always the whole person seen from a particular angle." As for the πνεῦμα (the Spirit), neither is this used to designate a constituent part of man: "By the πνεῦμα we understand the whole man as God speaks to him . . . . From that moment man becomes a Person, for it is a personal relationship into which he enters with God."[12]

And further, "It is characteristic of Christianity that choice is made not of principles but of a person, of the living God, of Christ. It does indeed bring with it all the moral principles that can be discovered by reason. But it makes us something more than mere machines applying principles: it makes us persons."[13]

Motive

One of the most common motives that restricts the involvement of the Holy Spirit in the conduct of theological inquiry is the desire to establish either the written words of Scripture or the religious experiences of persons as the *only* adequate data base for theology. I refer to these as "bibliolatry" and "charismania", respectively.

Bibliolatry. Much of the evangelical literature is filled with statements that any experience must be checked against the Bible as ultimate authority. This is a main thrust of the Credibility Model, which gives Christian psychologists an opportunity to enhance their credibility so they will be listened to in the evangelical subculture. But I am not saying all this is wrong. What I want to point out is that whereas I would agree that the Bible is, across all human situations and conditions, the universally clearest and therefore the most legitimate or authoritative of God's revelations,[14] the truths that it reveals must be *experienced* (read), as must the truths revealed by "religious experiences". Technically, reading Scripture is also a religious experience. So what we are doing is checking one experience against another kind of experience, where both are susceptible to error (the experiencing, human aspect, not the object of the experiencing, the divine) but the basis for one has more functional authority or legitimate power.

Reading Scripture is one experience; believing what I read, applying it to my life, and committing myself to it over time as truth for me are other experiences. Yet what is usually implied is that the Bible just sits there like prearranged alphabet soup. It just is, and experience starts after we read it. And then we check our experience against the Bible, the complex against the simple. That sounds right, but it is not quite right. I think it is an affront to God.

When we forget that reading Scripture is not so simple but rather quite complicated (both contaminated and enriched) by our feelings and our own thoughts, and that even the major translations vary significantly in places, the Bible becomes "The Living Bible", and the Bible "speaks".[15] We begin to worship the Bible itself, disregarding the Word behind the words. That is when the Bible becomes an Idol.

To me, the words are "nothing" but the Word is everything. That is to say, the purpose of the written words of the Bible is for God to show through, not for the Bible to draw attention to itself. "Oh send Thy Spirit, Lord, Now unto me, That He may touch my eyes And make me see: Show me the truth concealed Within Thy Word, And in Thy book revealed I see the Lord."[16]

We might say that the Reformation delivered us from a "papal Gospel", but bibliolatry has now given us a "paper Gospel". I think a corrective is needed, and that corrective could be called a "person Gospel". Rather than an object relating to paper, we would have a person relating to Person.

Rather than making belief in a theological conclusion about the Bible foundational to believing its content, the focus should be on the process itself of believing.

> Believing begins to look as if it has an armory of reasons in reserve; so one believes, then, not because of the attractiveness of Jesus or out of dire need or because of a chastened consciousness seeking forgiveness; instead the theology is like a system of warrants, a passel of guarantees, that shows you that the verses are true, and therefore believable . . . . [But] belief is not a starting point; instead, it is like a capacity rather slowly achieved by a Christian living in daily prayer, sacrificial obedience, devoted conformity to a variety of other scriptural teachings. [17]

This is exactly the point I am making about integration. *Integration is not a starting point;* instead, it is a process of sacrificial obedience to God through devoted conformity to His truths.

I have been deliberately analyzing bibliolatry rather than charismania. That is because the literature is unbalanced in the other direction. But the same thing applies. Both the Bible and religious experiences must be initially experienced to ultimately become truth for me — again, that is not needed to verify their claim as truth, but it is needed to establish their claim on me. Both are subject to "easy believism", whereby belief is a guaranteed starting point instead of a process of sacrificial obedience to God. The easy-believer says "I believed", instead of "I am believing"; in marriage, that translates into "I married my wife 15 years ago", instead of "I am marrying my wife every day of our life together."

Neither bibliolatry nor charismania provides an adequate motive for doing theology. The motive I have been suggesting as a corrective is simply the whole person in the presence of God.

Method

Referring back to Figure 3, in Chapter Three, it appears from the right-hand column that God "speaks" only through the Bible. God speaking through religious experiences other than reading the Bible does not seem to have a place. It will be recalled that psychology as a human science did not seem to have a place in the diagram either, so I suggested the need for a middle column. Now I would like to suggest the need for a fourth column, this time for the general category of religious experiences.

I have provided a more complete methodological flow chart for theological inquiry in Figure 7, as I did for psychological inquiry in Figure 5 in Chapter Three. It might be recalled that in Figure 4 in Chapter Three, I listed two kinds of theological inquiry, "scientific" and "humanistic". These can also be called, as in Figure 7, "transactional" and "experiential".

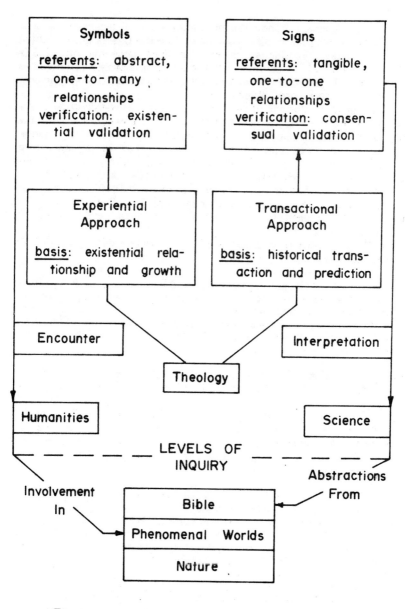

Figure 7.

49

Experiential Approach. The left-hand side of Figure 7 depicts the flow of experiential theological inquiry. Essentially, it accomplishes the existential validation (defined in Chapter Three) of a direct encounter with God (a religious experience). In contrast, the transactional approach accomplishes the consensual validation (corporate confirmation) of a once-removed interpretation of the words of Scripture.

The personal transformation half of the existential validation process that is involved here is primarily focused either on one's inner experience of the grace of God and repentance (according to the "official" Reformation tradition), or on every aspect of one's outward way of life and discipleship (according to the Anabaptist Reformation tradition). The contrast is exemplified by how two complementary features of baptism are incorporated by each tradition. The former views baptism as primarily a public statement of "I have accepted Jesus," or as a covenant with God. For the latter, the public statement expands to " . . . and I will *follow* Jesus," and the covenant is also with fellow believers.

Regarding religious experiences as direct encounters with God, Morton Kelsey notes that

> . . . most modern theologians are still caught, without really knowing it, by a thesis that no longer appears to hold water. Academic theology is still struggling with the idea that anything in our religion which claims to be a direct contact with reality other than the physical — i.e. symbols, myths, experiences, and all — comes only from the childhood of man, and represents only his effort to explain something that he was not rational or mature enough to understand.[18]

Consequently, Kelsey argues, modern theologians have not developed a formal methodology for direct inquiry into encounters with divine reality in and of themselves.

In fact, both extremes of modern theological inquiry — the dispensationalists and the demythologizers — " . . . are equally convinced that God has no contact with living individuals."[19] For example, the former are persuaded that God allowed such encounters with Himself as visions and healings only by a special dispensation, to

> . . . establish the people of Israel and, through them, the Church of Christ. Then he withdrew this dispensation and the normal order was restored . . . . [In our lives,] the Holy Spirit is not intended to be the giver of these experiences . . . , but is only sent to give the conviction that they did happen . . . . One's relation to God, then, is not a matter of a divine-human encounter, of two realities coming into confrontation, but rather a one-way street of the Word of God slipping into man's mind and instructing this part of him . . . .[20]

It is true that experiential theology does not have a sophisticated methodology, but I do not think that is entirely because of denial of direct contact with divine reality. Rather, the large number of theologians between the extremes who actually do give credence to the existential reality of the Holy Spirit in people's lives have not developed a sophisticated methodology because of what I have said under *Motive* above. Instead of inquiring directly into a religious experience itself, they merely check the validity of its occurrence against the written words of Scripture.

So, "... the church has relied on authority and doctrine, on theological understanding about [religious] experiences, instead of trusting the experiences themselves."[21] Kelsey, however, is trying to correct that, by offering a comprehensive historical, psychological, philosophical, and theological framework — based on the insights of Carl Jung — for trusting those intuitive, visionary, mystical experiences that are unapproachable by ordinary sense experience.

Another contemporary approach to religious experience is provided by Donald Gelpi.[22] In his consideration of the variables that structure experience in general, "the place of affectivity in the human encounter with the Holy", and "the present experiential accessibility of God", Gelpi formulates a general developmental model for dealing with human experience and applies it to religious experience.

Gelpi's book is primarily a complexly detailed elaboration of Christian conversion, which he defines as the lifelong Christian transformation of natural affective, intellectual, and moral experiential growth. Accordingly, he makes extensive use of the psychology of James, Jung, and Piaget, with supplementary help from Allport, Kohlberg, Kübler-Ross, Maslow, May, Merleau-Ponty, and Rogers, among others. Gelpi also analyzes what he calls "developmental mysticism", by situating several religious experiences such as glossolalia, visionary experience, prayer, and prophecy within his emergent model of Christian conversion.

Transactional Approach. Looking back at Figure 7, it is evident that the transactional approach is basically scientific in orientation: its findings are interpretations that are verified by consensus (hypotheses that become axiomatic postulates by corporate agreement — perhaps leading to the formation of a new denomination?) for the purpose of prediction (of the futility of the ungodly life and the fruit of the godly life, and of the fruition of eschatological events). It is also clear in the following, if we substitute the words "transactional theology" and "experiential theology" for "natural science" and "phenomenology":[23]

[T]he style of causal thinking in [transactional theology] is such that the attainment of knowledge is identical to possession of an inert and everlasting truth; for [experiential theology], critical thinking leads to a renewal in man's knowledge .... For [transactional theology], the absence of an absolute is threatening; for [experiential theology], the absence of the absolute in the traditional sense is openness to the truth. Causal thinking demands absolute evidence, otherwise how can we know things for certain? In [experiential theology], certitude is discovered only within the context

51

of interrogation. [Transactional theology] wants to persuade its community and society in general of the validity of its doctrines; [experiential theology] wants to call the community into question, to awaken a critical attitude that will sensitize its members to their limits, their presuppositions, their blind side. Perhaps the whole difference in style can be summarized as follows: [transactional theology] holds out *the* truth so that all men may submit to it; [experiential theology] presents a truth to be examined for its relevance to the examiner.

I believe that both approaches are very appropriate and fit well within an overall evangelical approach.[24] Some people have tended to split them apart, however, into the good guys and the bad guys, the literal types and the liberal types. If "liberal" refers to one's handling of Scripture, I personally would not affirm such activity. If it refers to inquiry into God's existential revelation (religious experiences), though, I am all for it. The latter is the case with the following, where compared with literal (antithetical categories, hearing, reasoning, moderation/tradition, preservation/standards, order, security, and stability), liberal refers to dialectical process, sensing, feeling, risk-taking, exploring, spontaneity, freedom, and creativity.[25] Or simply, the literal approach is most concerned with the Bible's veracity; the liberal approach is most concerned with our response to God.

The literal, transactional approach has several subtypes — the philological method, the typological method, and the allegorical method.[26] *The philological* (or historical-grammatical) *method* combines the historical background, cultural context, and grammatical interpretation of a passage of Scripture to discover its obvious central truth. It is the most literal of the transactional methods. *The typological method* highlights persons, things, or events in an Old Testament passage that naturally illustrate a passage in the New Testament, in order to forecast the age to come.

The allegorical method begins to move into an area of more hidden than obvious meanings, of reading meanings into the Bible more than reading meanings out of the Bible. Basically, this method (a) begins with Scripture and attempts to contemporize it, or (b) begins with an assumption or prior theological conclusion and looks back into Scripture for a passage that gives it divine significance or justification. A fourth hermeneutical method, which I would not regard as literal, moves much further into the area of hidden meanings. *The mythological method* unmasks the popular folklore character of a passage in order to recover its original existential meaning. This method is most popular with those employing the Convertibility Model of conceptual relation.

What can be done to more completely incorporate humanness and thereby more significant involvement of the Holy Spirit into the conduct of transactional theological inquiry? For one thing, we can acknowledge that reading the Bible is a whole-person event, affected just as much by personal feelings as by "purely" mental acts. Although this simply reveals the fact that what the Bible "says" may actually be more what the theologian "sees", it also opens up more communication channels for the Holy Spirit to give the true sense of the text. For another thing, we can insure that whichever method(s) one employs be "multi-perspectival".

Multi-perspectival method. No method(s) of hermeneutics should confine the truths of the Bible tò the limits of a white American male perspective. Letting the human condition in its broadest scope provide the framework for doing theology would be to combine Black theology, Third World liberation theology, feminist theology, and the bulk of theology that has been written out of male experience into a rich overall openness to the leading of the Spirit into God's truth.[27]

Charles Kraft emphasizes from an anthropological standpoint that different perspectives on the same data yield different understandings and interpretations, all of which may be valid, and that a cross-cultural approach to interpreting Scripture prevents us from falling into the trap of absolutizing some form of culture or relativizing the Lord. "Theologians . . . have been too prone to generalize on the basis of experience within a few closely-related (western) cultures."[28] The corrective is obviously an Afro-, Asio-, Latino-, . . . informed theology.

The importance of an Afro-informed theology, for example, is clear from the following critique by one of my students: "The distinction is made among culture, art, religion, etc. for the sake of white minds, because traditionally the Black man's religion, music, art, etc. were all a part of one entity. Consequently, in the Black man's mind, his expressions to his god(s) (God) and his relationship to his fellow-tribesmen were all one and the same thing, which eventually came together to be known as the ability to express *soul.*"[29] It is even clearer when one considers the "honky hermeneutic": " . . . a way of interpreting Scripture that prevents, obscures, or omits certain truths that show God's concern for the dispossessed."[30]

Latino-informed theology, or liberation theology, while also taking up the cause of the dispossessed, gives us an excellent example of an approach to Scripture from a cultural context other than our own. The methodology that is involved is most thoroughly and profoundly elaborated upon by Jon Sobrino, in a book that many believe puts to rest once and for all the common criticism that liberation theology is merely a thinly veiled apology for a Marxist analysis of society. According to Sobrino, the paradigm of liberation is the resurrection of Jesus; the pathway to liberation is the life of Jesus. Further, the basis for liberation theology is the Bible, with its methodological roots being in the historical Jesus (referring to the concrete and relational rather than abstract and doctrinal features of His life — action, not theory) as viewed from the horizon of the present-day Latin American situation of oppression, injustice, and exploitation.[31]

In addition to racial and cultural correctives, the feminist corrective is also needed to broaden the traditional white American male theological perspective. Consider the following:

... the interpretation of Gen. 3:16 has had a history something like this: Men of old found a phrase here that seemed to have to do with woman's relation to her husband, but it was beyond their comprehension. Unconsciously these men of olden time have consulted their own ideas of what a wife *should be*, in her relation to her husband, and inserted those ideas into their interpretation. The interpretation has been accepted by other men, without challenge, because it conformed to their unsanctified wishes, and handed on from generation to generation, until it became weighty through "tradition" . . . . Prejudice blinds men, even in their treatment of the Word of God, if a faulty rendering coincides with their preconceptions.[32]

We have seen through the course of this chapter that the Bible is too big in some people's hands and, conversely, that it is too small in other people's hands. My purpose has been to encourage us to let the Bible be as big as it is, without reducing it to the size of our own limited perspectives. The most significant involvement of the Holy Spirit in theological inquiry will come to pass with the inclusion of as much of humanity as possible. And I have touched on only three of the many relevant perspectives in such a multi-perspectival approach.

With the help of at least Black theology, liberation theology, and feminist theology, we will better understand God's continuous working throughout history. "Should the theological process consist simply of studying what great theologians of the past have produced? Not entirely . . . . [We] should honor the theologians of the past by following their example *in our context* rather than by simply passing along their products from one generation to the next."[33] And in our day, the twentieth century, our context is a world-wide context that includes almost all of humanity! Clearly, there is much, much work to be done.

Notes

1. Inspired by Otto, *The Idea of the Holy*, Appendix XI, "The *Mysterium Tremendum* in Robertson and Watts", pp. 220, 221.

2. See Maurice Merleau-Ponty, *The Primacy of Perception and Other Essays on Phenomenological Psychology, the Philosophy of Art, History and Politics,* trans. James M. Edie. Evanston, Illinois: Northwestern University, 1964.

3. Albert Einstein, "Letter to Jacques Hadamard". In E. Ghiselin (Ed.), *The Creative Process.* New York: Mentor, 1952. P. 43.

4. Francis A. Schaeffer, *Pollution and the Death of Man: The Christian View of Ecology.* Wheaton, Illinois: Tyndale House, 1970. P. 56.

5. Heinrich Emil Brunner, *God and Man: Four Essays on the Nature of Personality,* trans. David Cairns. London: Student Christian Movement, 1936.

6. Ibid. Probably the most thorough attempts in the modern literature to restore the balance between the rational and the nonrational, by elucidating the latter, are the works of Rudolph Otto and Morton Kelsey.

7. Viktor E. Frankl, *The Unconscious God.* New York: Simon and Schuster, 1975. P. 39.

8. May, *Love and Will.*

9. Ibid., p. 218.

10. Abraham J. Heschel, *The Prophets: An Introduction* (Vol. 1). New York: Harper & Row, 1962. P. 192.

11. *The Living Bible.* Wheaton, Illinois: Tyndale House, 1971. Isaiah 63:17. See also Romans 9:18.

12. Tournier, *The Meaning of Persons,* p. 163.

13. Ibid., pp. 215, 216.

14. As in psychology we must be concerned with the nature of the primary object of our study, the person — i.e. human nature — in theology we must likewise concern ourselves with the nature of our primary object of study, the Bible. One view of the latter, for example, is that " . . . we must . . . have a doctrine of the Scriptures which is of the same heartbeat as the theology of the cross. In the words of the British theologian Thornton, God's written Word is in the form of humiliation just as the Son of God in his incarnation. It too shares the brokenness, the servanthood, the masking of the divine glory as the incarnate Son. Or in the thought of the Dutch Old Testament scholar K. H. Miskotte (*When the Gods Are Silent*), Yahweh of the Old Testament leads a hidden, mysterious existence, for he alone will be worshipped and adored. And we dare not have a version of Scripture that betrays the nature in which Yahweh encounters man" — Bernard Ramm, "Misplaced Battle Lines", *The Reformed Journal,* 1976 (July-August), 37, 38.

Another, very important example, is a consideration of biblical authority. It occurs to me that the Bible, as part of God's creation, holds a particular positional authority and also has a particular functional authority within the totality of Creation. The positional side of the Bible's authority, however, is usually overemphasized at the expense of its functional side. I therefore think it is important to emphasize the latter when one is experiencing authority, e.g. reading the Bible. That is, the Bible has functional authority or legitimate power over me when I encounter God through its pages. The authority which is the basis for the functional authority of the Bible, however, inheres only in the living God. Authority, then, does not ultimately inhere in the thing I submit to that brings me into contact with the living God, the author of all things, the only ultimate authority.

My thinking on the interplay of these two aspects of biblical authority has been enriched by G. C. Berkouwer's alternative to the traditional Hodge/Warfield *rationalism* (dogmatic theoretical proofs of the Bible's divine character) — liberal *subjectivism* (nonliteral, experiential emphases on the human element of Scripture) polarization. With historical roots in the thinking of Augustine and Calvin, Berkouwer's alternative is that the Bible's authority is acknowledged (although *not* derived) through our Holy Spirit-aided experience of God's authority in our lives mediated through the Bible. We accept the Bible's functional authority, then, because of our experience of its saving message of Jesus, not because of some other theme found in its pages or some prior theoretical statement about its position in some hierarchy of authority. See G. C. Berkouwer, *Holy Scripture,* trans. Jack B. Rogers. Grand Rapids: William B. Eerdmans, 1975.

15. "[A] text cannot be made to speak to us until what it says has been understood" — E. D. Hirsch, Jr., *Validity in Interpretation.* New Haven: Yale University, 1967. P. 210; "Words do not mean; they do not say; people mean and say something or other with them" — Paul L. Holmer, "Contemporary Evangelical Faith: An Assessment and Critique". In D. F. Wells & J. D. Woodbridge (Eds.), *The Evangelicals: What They Believe, Who They Are, Where They Are Changing.* New York: Abingdon, 1975. P. 72. In sum, "Every theology is an attempt to decode a religious experience" — whether the experience is reading the Bible or speaking in tongues — Donald L. Gelpi, *Experiencing God: A Theology of Human Emergence.* New York: Paulist, 1978. P. 5.

16. Mary Ann Lathbury, "Break Thou the Bread of Life".

17. Holmer, "Contemporary Evangelical Faith", pp. 83, 84.

18. Morton Kelsey, *Encounter with God: A Theology of Christian Experience.* Minneapolis: Bethany Fellowship, 1972. P. 49. The appropriateness of Kelsey's strongly stated critique is explained well by E. Glenn Hinson, "Luxuriant Garden of Spirits and Images", *Sojourners,* 1979 (June), 29, 30: "For many years now, Morton Kelsey has been the best informed and most articulate Christian advocate of an expansive interpretation of an approach to reality."

19. Ibid., p. 33.

20. Ibid., pp. 30, 31.

21. Ibid., p. 24.

22. Gelpi, *Experiencing God.*

23. Giorgi, "Phenomenology and the Foundations of Psychology", pp. 322, 323.

24. I must caution, however, against an over-enthusiastic *transactionalism.* "Theology is not, as the old manuals had it, 'the science of God and things divine'; properly speaking, it is not about God, but about the mystery of God's relationship to the world . . . . [However,] is [the Mystery] completely contained, as it were, in the events of salvation history? Or would it be better to say that the saving events are contained in *it*? Are Jesus's death and resurrection, for example, the only communication of Atonement? Or is Atonement a vast Mystery of which Jesus's Death and Resurrection are just a single true, full, effective, preeminent communication? Obviously, we opted for the former. We assumed that the Mystery was contained in the transactions by which we learned about it

— that it could safely be spoken of as if it were operative only in the *pieces of business* presented to us in the revelation . . . . The Bible [itself] is indeed God's Word Written, and it most infallibly contains all things necessary for salvation. But it is also a thing. It is not the Mystery . . . " — Robert Farrar Capon, *Hunting the Divine Fox: Images and Mystery in Christian Faith*. New York: Seabury, 1974. Pp. 43, 108, 133.

25. Richard J. Coleman, *Issues of Theological Warfare: Evangelicals and Liberals*. Grand Rapids: William B. Eerdmans, 1972. Further rapprochement, among contending factions within just the literal approach, is encouraged by Coleman, Clark Pinnock, and others in the excellent "Symposium on Inerrancy", *Journal of the American Scientific Affiliation*, 1979, *31*, 65-88.

26. The following descriptions come from Bernard Ramm, *Protestant Biblical Interpretation: A Textbook of Hermeneutics*. Grand Rapids: Baker Book House, 1970.

27. Nancy Hardesty, "Toward a Total Human Theology", *Sojourners* (Suppl.), 1977 (Jan.), 58, 59. An excellent collection of perspectives on the Gospel from Black, feminist, Asian American, Native American, and Hispanic American experience is provided by Gerald H. Anderson and Thomas F. Stransky (Eds.), *Mission Trends No. 4: Liberation Theologies in North America and Europe*. New York and Grand Rapids: Paulist and William B. Eerdmans, 1979.

28. Charles H. Kraft, "The Process Not the Product". Unpublished paper, 1976, p. 12.

29. Joshua Sands, personal communication, October, 1976.

30. Clarence L. Hilliard, "The Honky Hermeneutic", *The Other Side*, 1976 (May-June), 66-72.

31. Jon Sobrino, *Christology at the Crossroads: A Latin American Approach*, trans. John Drury. Maryknoll, New York: Orbis Books, 1978. The *basis* for liberation theology highlights the "hermeneutic circle", which is a process similar to the process of integration. That is, much as embodiment completes and in turn verifies a conceptual relation, the lived examples of the historical Jesus guide Latin Americans in analyzing their own lives, and their own lived situation in turn provides a framework for analyzing and verifying their conclusions about the main thrust of Jesus' life.

The *perspective* of liberation theology is formed not by moralizing or intellectualizing about, but by living within. In other words, " . . . dogmas guarantee the truth *about* Christ. But if Christian individuals and Christian communities are to have *real first-hand knowledge of Christ*, . . . then they simply must reconsider Christ from the standpoint of their own situation and activity" (p. xxi) and incorporate the radical truth of Christ's existence into their own lives. This is very similar to the Anabaptist tradition: "The only way to get to know Jesus is to follow after him in one's own real life; to try to identify oneself with his own historical concerns; and to try to fashion his kingdom in our midst . . . . Following Jesus is the precondition for knowing Jesus" (p. xiii).

The *main contribution* of liberation theology to theology in general, in terms of product, is the conclusion that the central focus of Jesus' ministry is proclamation of the coming of the kingdom, denunciation of injustice as the epitome of sin, partiality toward the poor and the oppressed, and unmasking of alienating powers. In terms of process, the main contribution is in shifting " . . . the basic issue from the content of theology to the precondition for doing any Christian theology. When we insist that theology can be done only within the context of praxis, we are saying that people can understand and appreciate the Jesus who sends the Spirit only if they live a life in accordance with that Spirit. When we stress the full realization of the kingdom of God, we are saying that this mysterious, utopian reality is the ultimate horizon of theology; though it ever remains ahead of us and we are incapable of realizing it fully, it is the deepest source of our life and being because it points us toward our future" (p. xxv).

32. Bushnell, *God's Word to Women*, paragraph 112.

33. Kraft, "The Process Not the Product", p. 3.

CHAPTER V

AN ANTHROPOLOGICAL BASIS FOR INTEGRATION

In Chapter Two, I reasoned that wherever the integration of two disciplines is concerned, the bottom line for the Christian is always the activity of God. Since two disciplines can come together most fruitfully if there is some basic similarity in their respective research processes, I defined both psychology and theology as particular ways of living with God so as to know His truths. This not only opens up both disciplines to the activity of the Holy Spirit, but potentially incorporates that activity into every area of the research process: (a) choosing the methodology; (b) generating the data; (c) applying the results.

Knowing God, then, is the purpose of integration. Since communicating with Him is therefore of crucial importance, similarity with God, in order to make communicating with Him possible, is the main crux of integration. And the similarity that we have with God is our humanness, or person/spirit dimension. This is the key to a Spirit-filled psychology as well as to a Spirit-filled theology. It is what turns it all on. The ingredients of such Spirit-filled inquiries, which are the conclusions of Chapters Three and Four, are summarized in Figure 8.

	PSYCHOLOGY	THEOLOGY
Mentality:	Generosity and reverence toward human experience	The undiminished humanness of the whole person
Motive:	Christ's active intervention in the research process	The whole person in the presence of God
Method:	Psychology as a human science	Multi-perspectival theological inquiry

Figure 8.

Because of the obvious centrality of the human person to the entire integration process, we must now turn our attention to just what a person is. Considering the importance of human-divine encounter in the integration process, what advantage is there to a nonexclusionary, nonfragmented view of the physical/psychological/spiritual makeup of persons?

The study of the whole person, or the use of any word to refer to the whole person, is best termed "anthropological", after the root word "anthropos" meaning the entirety of human being. In looking closely at our total personhood, we will naturally have to deal with several key anthropological terms. And since I am promoting the idea that our personhood and spiritual nature are by definition the same — person and spirit are one — the anthropological terminology used will have to be clearly defined to give the idea credibility.

Many people, however, are not convinced that key anthropological terms should be used to refer to the whole person. Talking about "the wholeness of the person", for them, is making sure that all of the physical fragments, all of the psychological fragments, and all of the spiritual fragments are included in the discussion. That is not what I mean by wholeness. All of the "parts" of our humanness *represent*, do not just refer to, the whole person. We do not add up parts to get a whole — rather, each part is in its own special way a representation of the whole. Each distinguishable aspect of humanness is the whole person, each in its own way.[1] The purpose of this chapter will be to reveal how this is so and how it affects human-divine encounter.

Terminology

Body

A high view of body has been a basic thrust of this book. Body is more than meets the eye; body is meaning-giving and meaning-receiving. Body is more than a mere container for soul; body is a communication system. Body is more than "having a body"; I am a body.

Body is the person's openness toward and involvement in his/her phenomenal world. Body extends beyond itself, as depicted by the term "body english". "Just as a golfer feels in his body, in the position of his feet, and in the muscular sense of his swing, the whole scene in front of him, so do we bodily experience the complexity of our situations and interactions."[2] "[T]he bodily dimension of man, far from being a prison house or a barrier, serves as the self's exclusive mode of experience and expression, the way of communication, communion, and community."[3]

Arnold Come regards body as the locale of God and the person's life together. "[M]an's bodily dimension is what permits him simultaneously to be spirit or person distinct *from* God and yet to be in encounter and communion *with* God."[4] The result is, in the vulgar form, "God in the gut": "Behold, Thou doest desire truth in the inward parts, and in the hidden part Thou wilt make me know wisdom;"[5] "But whoso hath this world's good, and seeth his brother have need, and shutteth up his bowels *of compassion* from him, how dwelleth the love of God in him?"[6]

"For if your whole body is full of light, with no part of it in shadow, it will all be radiant — it will be like having a bright lamp to give you light."[7]

Mind

According to a standard reference,

biblical conceptions of psychology lack analytical and technical precision. Both OT and NT focus attention on man's concrete and total relationship to God, and where psychological terms do appear their intention seems to be emphasis rather than a concern to divide or compartmentalize man's activity. For this reason, no consistent pattern of terminology can be determined in either Testament . . . . What is obvious as one surveys the complexity of Biblical terminology is that no one term occupies an exclusive meaning, nor is one term alone used to indicate the faculty of reflection or cognition . . . . The being of man is a united whole and his reflective or cognitive faculties are never isolated from his total being. On the one hand, the Bible locates the center of man's being in those physical organs where man existentially grasps the reality of God and the world . . . At the same time, the Bible does specifically call attention to man as a thinking being.[8]

I pointed out in Chapter Three, while discussing intentionality, that meanings are never purely intellectual. Mind " . . . is not a special transcendent faculty but is precisely the whole man in unified . . . knowing . . . ."[9]

Will. A term that is often associated with mind is will.

Neither the principal terms used in Scripture to indicate acts of human will, nor the less frequently used terms, indicate a "faculty" of will, or a specific "power" of willing . . . . It becomes evident . . . that they depict man as an agent with responsibility for his acts rather than denoting a discrete faculty, "the will", and . . . that it is accordingly *the man* who chooses or desires or refuses, rather than "his will".[10]

Soul

Richard Bube utilizes systems theory as a way of looking at terms like soul.

[C]onsider the system that we recognize as an automobile. This system has various subsystems: fuel pump, spark plugs, . . . wheels, etc. Each of these subsystems has smaller sub-subsystems and basic parts. Put them all together in a particular patterned interaction and the automobile emerges. When one sits behind the wheel of a well-designed and attractive car and experiences the exhilaration of being in control of a swiftly-moving powerful vehicle, one recognizes the systems properties of an automobile. Being a deadly missile on the highway in the hands of a careless driver is also a systems property of the automobile.[11]

Soul is not a property of an isolated part, nor is it merely an illusion. Soul is, according to the metaphor, a patterned interaction of living matter.

Bube further hypothesizes as to the changeability of soul. A newly created life-system has a soulish property at every moment of its life span commensurate with the development of the entire system. At conversion, a change process is begun whereby the "I" before conversion is progressively put to death and the "I" after conversion is progressively born anew. "Conversion not only 'saves' a man's soul, it also changes it."[12] And finally, "if a soul is to exist after the death of the body, it must be a soul newly created by God for a new mode of existence, for the soul that we see, experience, and deal with in this life is intimately and indissolubly related to the health and life of the body . . . . [T]he Christian hope is in God's work of resurrection, in which he will create a new life-system for each life-system that has existed in this world."[13]

Bruce Reichenbach has also dealt with what we might call the reification and re-creation of soul hypotheses, and helpfully, with two primary criticisms of the latter. First, "If soul is not some kind of entity, then the person has no spiritual dimension." Reichenbach's conclusion:

> The spiritual dimension of man has to do with his *relationship* to God and his fellow man, a relationship which has been severed through the self-assertive activity of the individual. It is a relationship of love, obedience, trust, giving, faith, and of hope. But this relationship and the development of these qualities is not dependent upon the possession of some sort of spiritual entity; rather, the relationship and disrelationship deal with the whole man. Love, trust, obedience are things that I do with my body as much as with my mind. Indeed, their manifestation cannot be isolated in any one part of my being; they exist in my entire being-in-the-world.[14]

Second, "If soul is not an entity, then the person has no life after death." Reichenbach concludes, after an informative discussion, that soul was reified mainly to guarantee human immortality, but that if any part of a person does not die but lives on, then the teaching of Scripture that the whole person dies is inaccurate. Further,

> under [the re-creation view] immortality (literally, not-dying) is not possible; the individual does die. What is possible is life after death. Whereas under [the reification view], death is not possible, though immortality is provided for by the existence of a soul-entity which does not die. Thus, if one adopts a [re-creation] view of man, one must be careful to distinguish life after death from immortality; only the former is possible under this view. Hence, one should be careful about his language, no longer speaking about the immortality of man, but rather about his life after his death.[15]

Soul, then, is the personality of one's life-system; it is the vitality of one's being-in-the-world. It is, especially within the Black cultural context, the passion of one's bodily openness toward and involvement in one's phenomenal world.

Spirit

Extending Reichenbach's comment above, and borrowing from Kierkegaard, Barth, and Buber, I would define spirit as the synthesis of the bodily, the mental, and the soulish that is our capacity to respond to the address of the Holy Spirit through relationship with others and the Other. It is our overall capacity for communication, comprised of both sensitivity (feeling) and sensibility (reason).

> [I]t is so impossible to identify man essentially with [the bodily or the soulish] that man must be identified with the *unity* of the two as a third factor. This third dimen-

sion consists of man as self or spirit . . . . [However,] the spirit of man . . . [is] neither a third entity from some other world, seeking release to that other world, nor a synthesis that swallows up and blurs all distinctions. Rather, human spirit is a realized unity of the whole man that preserves, indeed is even posited on the grounds of, a continuing presence and operation of the bodily and soulish dimensions of the human self . . . . Man qua man, then, is a realized indissolvable unity of body and soul, denoted by the term "spirit", or, in contemporary language, "self" or "person" . . . . [A] part from that unique relation wherein the two have continuing significance, the human self, or spirit, or person can have no life or reality.[16]

People have always found it difficult to relate body, mind, soul, and spirit in a coherent fashion. Traditionally, body, mind, and spirit, for example, have been regarded as separate, noninteracting entities or layers of existence, with spirit and mind the only layers that communicate with God. I call this the Layer Model (see Figure 9). A more modern view is that spirit is the core of the person, manifesting itself outward through bodily and mental functions.[17] Only the spirit, then, however indirectly, communicates with the Spirit of God. I call this the Core Model (see Figure 9).

I believe a third model, what I would call the Unity Model, would be more accurate. In this model, as shown in Figure 9, spirit is equivalent to self or person, the indissolvable unity of body and mind, the overall capacity for communication with God. Because bodily and mental functions are equally part of spiritual being and each represents the entire person or spirit, body and mind together (not as separate entities) communicate with God. Or more precisely, human spirit communication is bodily/mental communication with the Holy Spirit.

Flesh. A term that is very similar to spirit is flesh. Quite simply, flesh is the whole person apart from the influence of the Holy Spirit, that is, spirit alienated from God. " '[T] he spirit indeed is willing but the flesh is weak' cannot be interpreted dualistically but must be a reference to the impotence of human spirit to realize itself by itself."[18] It is not my spirit can but my flesh cannot, but rather with God I can and without God I cannot![19]

Further, " . . . 'fleshly' indicates that the creaturely, finite, temporal dimension has become the ruling factor in a man's life and so is descriptive of the general tendency or direction of his life."[20]

Heart

In my brief discussion of will, above, I concluded that the whole person, not "the will", chooses or desires or refuses. This pervasively volitional or willing dimension of human being is what I think the biblical term "heart" means "The spirit is willing" is heart. And heart is " . . . not so much a matter of decision but of the whole cumulative tendency or direction of [one's] life."[21]

63

Layer Model

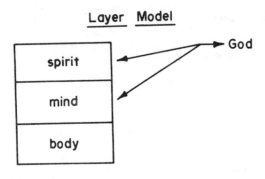

Core Model

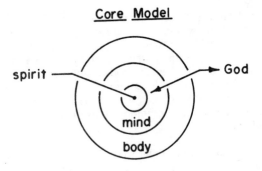

Unity Model

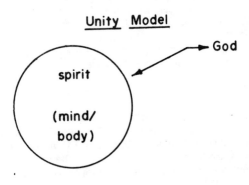

Figure 9.

"Return to Me with all your heart, fasting, and weeping and mourning, come! Rend your hearts and not your garments, and return to the Lord, your God."[22] Notice the bodily, soulish, and mental components of heart. To return to God, He wants all of me, not just "my thought life" or whatever. "But it was only with their words they followed him, not with their hearts."[23]

To worship God, He wants all of me, the physical as well as the cerebral. He wants *wholehearted worship* — the directing of my entire being toward Himself with praise and thanksgiving.

In praise we see how totally the emotions need to be brought into the act of worship. Worship that is solely cerebral is an aberration .... The Bible describes worship in physical terms. The root meaning for the Hebrew word we translate *worship* is "to prostrate." The word *bless* literally means "to kneel." *Thanksgiving* refers to "an extension of the hand." Throughout Scripture we find a variety of physical postures in connection with worship: lying prostrate, standing, kneeling, lifting the hands, clapping the hands, lifting the head, bowing the head, dancing and wearing sackcloth and ashes. The point is that we are to offer God our bodies as well as all the rest of our being. Worship is appropriately physical.

We are to present our bodies to God in worship in a posture consistent with the inner spirit in worship. Standing, clapping, dancing, lifting the hands, lifting the head are postures consistent with the spirit of praise. To sit still, looking dour, is clearly inappropriate for praise. Kneeling, bowing the head, lying prostrate are postures consistent with the spirit of humility. [But] we are quick to object to this line of teaching. "People have different temperaments," we argue. "That may appeal to emotional types, but I'm naturally quiet and reserved. It isn't the kind of worship that would meet my need." What we must see is that the real question in worship is not "what will meet my need?" The real question is "what kind of worship does God call for?" It is clear that God calls for wholehearted worship.[24]

In summary, whereas body is primarily intentionality and mind is primarily intention, heart is both intentionality and intentions. Whereas soul is the vitality of one's life, heart is the character of one's life. And whereas spirit is our unifying communication capacity, heart is our unifying shaping capacity. "Don't pile up treasures on earth .... But keep your treasure in heaven .... For wherever your treasure is, your heart will be there too! ... Set your heart first on his kingdom and his goodness ...."[25] That is precisely what integration is all about.

Human-Divine Encounter

Now, how does the anthropological terminology I have developed affect human-divine encounter so as to facilitate the development of a Spirit-filled psychology and a Spirit-filled theology?

Specifically, viewing body, mind, soul, and spirit, each in its own special way, as representative of the whole person gives us a very rich data base. Particularly if we see body as the exclusive locale for one's communication with God, and spirit as the indissolvable body/mind unity that is one's capacity for such communication, then we will see that human-divine encounter has an incalculable number of possibilities. No longer will we regard the Holy Spirit as limited to verbal-mental revelation only, and we will certainly have to change our psychological and theological inquiries (as described in Chapters Three and Four) to allow for our expanded recognition of the activity of the Holy Spirit.

More generally, "You will seek Me and find Me when you search for Me with all your heart."[26] This is the Lord's imperative for knowing Him. And this is how we can optimize human-divine encounter in our psychological and theological searching after His truths. But our search can go awry if we are out of fellowship with God — in relationship with Him but momentarily not communicating with Him (being fleshly).

The problem is compounded for the person who is not even in relationship with God — has not confessed Jesus Christ as Lord and Savior. Figure 10 illustrates the differences between being in relationship with God and being out of relationship with God, utilizing the key anthropological terminology developed in this chapter.

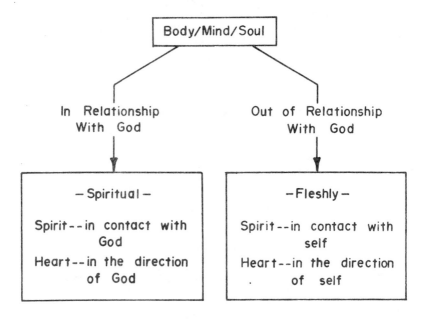

Figure 10.

66

There are basic distinctions between the fleshly or unregenerate person, human spirit in contact with "itself", and the spiritual or regenerate person, human spirit in contact with Holy Spirit. But it is important to note that

> ... there is nothing more in a regenerate man than in an unregenerate man, just as there is nothing more in a man who is walking in the right direction than in one who is walking in the wrong direction. In another sense, however, it might be said that the regenerate man is *totally* different from the unregenerate, for the regenerate life, the Christ that is formed in him, transforms every part of him .... [27]

Indwelling

If there is "nothing more" in the person in whom Christ is "formed", who is "filled with the Spirit", then what does "indwelling" mean? Indwelling must be understood, because it is the basis for Spirit-filled psychology and Spirit-filled theology. I think there are two metaphors that describe it best: it is a matter of breath, not blood; it is a matter of relationship, not injection.

Breath. Martin Buber very vividly protrays the first metaphor:

> Man speaks in many tongues — tongues of language, of art, of action — but the spirit is one; it is response to the You that appears from the mystery and addresses us from the mystery .... Spirit is not in the I but between I and You. It is not like the blood that circulates in you but like the air in which you breathe. Man lives in the spirit when he is able to respond to his You. He is able to do that when he enters into this relation with his whole being. [28]

Indwelling is the daily in-spiration celebrated by one of our great hymns: "Breathe on me, Breath of God, Fill me with life anew, That I may love what Thou dost love And do what Thou wouldst do. Breathe on me, Breath of God, Until my heart is pure, Until with Thee I will one will — To do and to endure. Breathe on me, Breath of God, Till I am wholly Thine, Till all this earthly part of me Glows with Thy fire divine." [29] It is also the *future* giving of spiritual life to the people of Israel, who cry out, " ... 'Our bones are dried up, our hope is lost ... ' ": "I will put breath into you, and you shall live .... I will put My Spirit within you, and you shall live .... " [30] And it is, at least partially, the *historic* act of Jesus breathing on the disciples and saying, "Receive the Holy Spirit." [31]

Relationship. The second metaphor is like that of a tool. When I use a hammer or a saw, I treat it not as an external object but as an extension of myself. *I* am hammering or sawing. In a primitive sense, I "dwell in" the tool when I use it, just as God "dwells in" me when He uses me for His good purpose. I like this metaphor better than that of the glove: I am a glove and He is the hand. Indwelling is being in relationship, not being in.

So when I "invite Jesus into my heart", He does not come inside my heart: the Holy Spirit does not inject Himself into my blood. The question is, how does He impact my life, and where does He do it? Quite simply, I desire Jesus to be the ruling factor in my life: desire is the how, and the direction of my life is the where.

Jesus summed it all up beautifully during His farewell discourse to His disciples.

> Do you not believe that I am in the Father and the Father is in me? . . . It is the Father who lives in me who carries out his work through me. You must believe me when I say that I am in the Father and *the Father is in me*. But . . . *I am going away to the Father* . . . . [A]nd I shall ask the Father to give you Someone else to *stand by you*, to *be with you* always. I mean the Spirit of truth, . . . [who] is with you now and is *in your hearts*. I am not going to leave you alone in the world — I am coming to you . . . .When that day comes, you will realize that *I am in my Father,* that *you are in me,* and *I am in you.* [32]

Jesus was "in" the Father, nevertheless He went away to be with the One who was already "in" Him, and we are "in" Jesus and thereby the Father because the Holy Spirit stands by us and with us. The Greek word for the Holy Spirit, *Paracletos*, means One called alongside to help. He is "in" our hearts, the flow of our daily existence — our life is His life. Or, back to the metaphor, Jesus (represented by the Holy Spirit) is the vine, and we are the branches.

Parenthetically, the metaphor similarly suggests a clarification for the inescapable psychological-theological confusion over the possible indwelling of evil spirits, or demon possession. "[S]uch language is not to be interpreted too spatially. The demons are spirits and are not inside of us, but rather are in a personal relation to us . . . . It would appear . . . that demons are 'in' people in various degrees of relationship . . . . "[33] Demon influence, perhaps, rather than possession as such.

It is important not to view indwelling as an injection. If it were, we would have the subversion of human personality and the perversion of the image of God.[34]

> Paul makes explicitly clear that the presence of the Spirit or of Christ . . . does not operate . . . dynamistically like a fluid welling up from subconscious depths to permeate and to comprise the content of all human life and action . . . . To the classic statement that "it is no longer I who live, but Christ who lives in me", he immediately adds, "the life I now live . . . I live by *faith* in the Son of God" (Gal. 2:20). And when he asks how "he who supplies the Spirit" works miracles among men he answers, "by hearing with *faith*" (Gal. 3:5). Christ (or the Spirit) is present, is our very life, only and always in the relational structure of *faith.*[35]

Faith is the glue that makes it all hold together. Faith is the bridge between the Holy Spirit and myself. Spirit-filled psychology and theology, then, are dependent upon, in Come's words, "the relational structure of faith" and "hearing with faith". To conclude this chapter, I will look first at the relational structure of faith as what makes communication with God by design possible, and second at hearing with faith — prayer — which is the communication itself.

Faith

I would agree with Viktor Frankl[36] that seeking out God and searching after His truths are not inborn tendencies, but I disagree with him that they are merely the result of a pre-given cultural mold that we are born into. Neither the person *nor* the culture is the initiator. Rather, God initially addresses *us* — *He* makes us aware at some level of awareness of His presence. Our initial seeking of Him and searching after His truths are in response to that communication. This is the Holy Spirit drawing us unto Himself, "the dialogue in the darkness of the unconscious", that I referred to at the end of Chapter Three.

After our initial response to God, we increasingly search for Him with all our heart as we continue believing, trusting, and obeying Him. One way I have found to understand this is to differentiate between the script of the drama and the stage upon which the drama is played out. The stage is historicity — the authenticity of the object of my faith, Jesus Christ. The script is faith itself — the reality of human-divine encounter. The following illustrates these two halves, the object and the reality, of faith: "[R]eal spirituality lies in the existential, moment-by-moment looking to the blood of Christ, and upon the basis of the work of Christ seeking and asking God in faith for a substantial reality in our relationship with Him . . . ."[37]

Our faith does not grow if we just keep nailing planks onto the stage by continuously rehearsing historicity — giving testimonies about when we first believed and arguing about the inerrancy of Scripture. I must say that these things are not all bad. But faith is ongoing and vital, so we must proceed to the drama itself. "Let us stop going over the same old ground again and again, always teaching those first lessons about Christ. Let us go on instead to other things and become mature in our understanding, as strong Christians ought to be."[38]

Types of faith. The drama of faith is depicted well by Nels Ferré.[39] The negative side of the script, "false faith", is of three kinds: fixation; fugitive; futile. *Fixation faith*, or dogmatism, is sitting the drama out. It is faith in a ready-made past, in ready-made sights not personally seen, in travel reports from previous participants in the drama. "When one set of doctrines is selected as alone leading to the goal, whereas countless others have indicated that they have proceeded with some success along quite different lines, ancestor worship is taking the place of divine worship."[40] Dogmatic adherence to the doctrines formulated by such great pilgrims as Luther, Calvin, or Wesley could actually, then, be little more than ancestor worship.

Fugitive faith, or escapism, is running away from the drama. It is faith in an imaginary future, demonstrated by constant shifting from one position to another. It is temporary allegiance to first one religion and then another, or first one cult and then another. *Futile faith*, or existential*ism*, is moving through the drama without moving anywhere. It is faith in the purely arbitrary or the completely absurd, or quite simply, faith in faith itself.

The positive side of the script, "true faith", is characterized by being flexible. *Flexible faith* is accepting the drama for what it is: ". . . doing what God is doing, and so giving up our plans for making history."[41] It is faith in what is never fully given nor beyond finding.

True faith is the whole-response of the person on the move in the direction of his/her treasure: it is the dynamic of heart, or heart on the move. Faith is the fuel. Faith *gives* direction; heart *is* the direction. Heart is the capacity to seek first God's kingdom and His righteousness; faith is doing it.

Faith is a total, preconceptual/conceptual response to one's phenomenal world. It is intentionality and intentions. The finality of faith, then, is not static, infallible conceptual knowledge, but organismic movement toward or basic trust in what is not fully seen. "Man does not need to know as God knows, but he needs to trust God within the failures of his sight as well as the sin of his life. Man above all else needs to trust the love of God."[42]

Prayer

"The relational structure of faith", the script of the drama, is based upon trusting God, and "hearing with faith", or communicating with God, takes place within that trust relationship. Communicating with God is prayer. Prayer within the context of integration, though, must not be restricted to verbal expression. It is a total orientation toward God; it is being prayer-full.

Being prayer-full is bodily/mentally stretching forth to God, orienting oneself toward Him, and drawing into consciousness the things of God. It is a way of life, not an event: "Be glad for all God is planning for you. Be patient in trouble, and prayerful always."[43] "Amen" is too often a mental period to a prayer-full process that should not be interrupted. In what ways is God communicating with us that we are not aware of? What doors is God trying to open, what truths is He trying to show us if we would only hear with faith, if we would only listen? Jesus said, to believers, "Behold I stand at the door and knock . . . ,"[44] and I am afraid the Holy Spirit is knocking on many of our doors that we do not even know are there.

Thomas Merton, in his final work, refers to "the contemplative orientation of emptiness" — the listening with one's entire being in silence and expectancy for the in-spiration of the grace of God — that is a dying to one's self-aspirations and to all "ways", that penetrates and enlivens every department of one's life.[45] Even the research department where, in a word, prayer is research.

Being prayerful always, including while in the laboratory doing research, depends heavily on one's ability to be silent, with an expectancy of hearing God. Sören Kierkegaard describes the process, in terms of one who has already become "the true man of prayer":

In proportion as he became more and more earnest in prayer, he had less and less to say, and in the end he became quite silent. He became silent — indeed, . . . he became a hearer. He had supposed that to pray is to speak; he learnt that to pray is not merely to be silent but to hear. And so it is; to pray is not to hear oneself speak, but it is to be silent, and to remain silent, to wait, until the man who prays hears God . . . . Not as though prayer always began with silence . . . , but when prayer has really become prayer it has become silence.[46]

Hearing God can also involve asking God, when the emphasis is on "emptiness", or being open to any response in the area of the petition, rather than being interested only in receiving what is requested. "Ask, and you will receive; seek, and you will find; knock, and the door will be opened"[47] — not ask and your will *receive*, but *ask* and you will receive. Asking is listening when it tunes one into an area of one's life so that God's will in that area may be heard. And hearing involves waiting for the Lord. It is His history, not mine. Again, Kierkegaard expresses it well:

The immediate person thinks and imagines that when he prays, the important thing, the thing he must concentrate upon, is that *God should hear* what *HE is praying for*. And yet in the true, eternal sense it is just the reverse: the true relation in prayer is not when God hears what is prayed for, but when the *person praying* continues to pray until he is *the one who hears*, who hears what God wills. The immediate person, therefore, uses many words and, therefore, makes demands in his prayer; the true man of prayer only *attends*.[48]

Attending to God's revelations is a process involving all of my humanness, all of my personhood. Responding to God's revelations, the other half of being prayerful always, also involves one's entire being. Therefore, responding prayerfully also need not be restricted to words. In fact, it can assume a variety of forms. "Prayer is the soul's sincere desire, Unuttered or expressed; The motion of a hidden fire That trembles in the breast. Prayer is the burden of a sigh, The falling of a tear, The upward glancing of an eye, When none but God is near."[49]

"Prayer . . . largely overflows the confines of the spoken language, although this fact is often forgotten in Protestant circles. There is the prayer of incense, of bells, of the dance, of gestures."[50] Consider the picture in II Samuel 6 of David and all the house of Israel dancing with all kinds of instruments, shouting and leaping, showing their joy before the Lord!

A quieter expression of responding to God is "groanings of the Spirit".[51] Jacques Ellul argues that this phrase has too often been interpreted as though the Holy Spirit added a little something to our prayer. In short, we pray, but not very well. Our prayer is incomplete, unsatisfactory. Fortunately, the Holy Spirit helps the situation by completing what we are unable to say. That is quite incorrect. It is the entire prayer which is the prayer of the Holy Spirit. If we conceive of prayer as language it is then that we do not know what to put into the discourse. It is nothing because it cannot have a content.[52]

Attending and responding to God — communication with Him; prayer — then, "... is not a language which makes possible the construction of a discourse. It takes place on an altogether different plane.... It is a form of life, the life with God. That is why it is not confined to the moment of verbal statement. The latter can only be the secondary expression of the relationship with God, an overflow from the encounter between the living God and the living person."[53] That is being prayer-full. And it is, as I said near the end of Chapter Two, the proper perspective on integrating God's truths in one's life and then writing about it.

Ellul concludes, and I will conclude, with the emphasis that prayer "... is not my little story, my fears and desires, which I have to tell to God.... It is the statement, the proclamation, in all of its aspects and directions (and consequently including also my fears and desires!), of the life led with the living God. It is not *my* life, of which he would know nothing, but the life which I receive from him, and which unfolds in a story with him."[54] It is the story of God's creation, told through His existential and propositional revelations, that unfolds with faith-full, prayer-full living with God that is the goal of a Spirit-filled psychology and a Spirit-filled theology. And it is possible if the conduct of our inquiries will just not deny or restrict our personhood.

Notes

1. The perspective on human being that emerges from this idea of wholeness, plus the idea that a whole person is not just an animal with something human or divine added, is provocatively outlined by Peter A. Bertocci, *Free Will, Responsibility, and Grace.* New York: Abingdon, 1957. Pp. 90-92. "A human being ... is not an animal with rationality added. He is not a mere plastic set of needs and wants, which allow him more possibility than animals enjoy. He is not an animal with more choices, made possible by his capacity for self-conscious reflection and symbolization. He is not an unconscious wasteland of nonmoral desires insecurely tied down by a superego which automatizes the prudential bargaining of his ego with the surrounding culture. Nor is Homo sapiens a creature who is one-third animal, one-third man, and one-third God ....

[The 'higher animal'] view, I believe, misconceives the nature of man by thinking of his human nature as something emerging from and added to animal structure. However, many persons, unsatisfied by this conception, [are] subject to the seduction of thinking of man as a fallen god. Man, they [say], may be an animal, yes, but he is also a god, for the spark of the divine in him is his hope and his despair. Man is a limited creature of space and time, but he is also a spirit disturbed by eternity in him; he is a self-transcendent being, forever goaded by stirrings which show that he is a denizen of two worlds, the eternal and the temporal. Yet despite the fact that there are many who propose this view as the pervading biblical view, we may wonder whether such views actually do justice to man. Should we keep on trying to think of man either as a higher animal or a fallen god? It seems to me that if we do we take our eyes off man himself and fit him either into a cozy divine economy or into a constricted scientific scheme.

The thesis I would defend is that man is what he is, neither animal nor god, that his society is neither that of an animal bewildered by new plasticity and capacity, nor a lost paradise. Our approach must see man as he is and not fit him into schemes either of evolution or of salvation. Man is not a complicated animal body; he is *his* body; man is not a partially divine mind; he is *his* mind; and to say that he is indissolubly mind and body seems to me to create more problems than it solves. Man must be seen as he is, a particular type of complex being, with certain kinds of activities, certain kinds of yearnings and cognitive capacities, and other functions which characterize him . . . . Following this procedure, and focusing on man as he experiences himself, we would suggest that man is a creature whose desires even are none of them like those of animals when seen *within the context of his whole being."*

2. Eugene T. Gendlin, "Focusing", *Psychotherapy: Theory, Research and Practice,* 1969, *6*, 8.

3. Come, *Human Spirit and Holy Spirit*, p. 41.

4. Ibid., p. 43.

5. *New American Standard Bible*, Psalm 51:6.

6. *The Holy Bible: King James Version*, I John 3:17.

7. Phillips, *The New Testament in Modern English*, Luke 11:36.

8. Donald M. Lake, "Mind". In M. C. Tenney (Ed.), *The Zondervan Pictorial Encyclopedia of the Bible* (Vol. 4). Grand Rapids: Zondervan Publishing House, 1975, 1976. Pp. 228, 229.

9. Come, *Human Spirit and Holy Spirit*, p. 78.

10. Arthur F. Holmes, "Will". In M. C. Tenney (Ed.), *The Zondervan Pictorial Encyclopedia of the Bible* (Vol. 5). Grand Rapids: Zondervan Publishing House, 1975, 1976. P. 931.

11. Richard H. Bube, *The Human Quest: A New Look at Science and the Christian Faith*. Waco, Texas: Word Books, 1971. P. 143.

12. Ibid., p. 149.

13. Ibid., pp. 147-149.

14. Bruce Reichenbach, "Life After Death: Possible or Impossible?" *Christian Scholar's Review*, 1973, *3*, 238.

15. Ibid., p. 243. See also Murray Harris, "Resurrection and Immortality: Eight Theses", *Themelios*, 1976, *1*, 50-55, and Oscar Cullmann, "Immortality of the Soul or Resurrection of the Dead?" In K. Stendahl (Ed.), *Immortality and Resurrection*. New York: Macmillan, 1965. Regarding the question of continuity between one's earthly relationship with God and one's recreated life with God, Donald MacKay reasons that it is a matter of the quality of the former that is preserved, by implication, in the memory of God and reembodied by the creative act of God. Resurrection, then, involves a recreated "sequel to our earthly career" that brings to eternal fruition the consequences of our present response to our Creator — Donald M. MacKay, "Brain Research and Human Responsibility". In C. F. H. Henry (Ed.), *Horizons of Science: Christian Scholars Speak Out*. New York: Harper and Row, 1978.

16. Come, *Human Spirit and Holy Spirit*, pp. 35, 37.

17. Paul Tournier, *The Whole Person in a Broken World*, trans. John and Helen Doberstein. New York: Harper & Row, 1964.

18. Come, *Human Spirit and Holy Spirit*, p. 76.

19. Rudolf Otto (*Religious Essays: A Supplement to "The Idea of the Holy"*, trans. Brian Lunn. London: Oxford University, 1931) places the battle between spirit and flesh into four stages, revealing how common interpretations progress from dualism to wholism: *reason* versus passion; *altruism* versus egoism (the first two stages divide the person in half, into conflicting capacities — psychic elements — for the suppression or liberation of the flesh in the literal sense, and are resolved merely by the dominant interest or inclination of one of the psychic halves); *obedience* to the law versus disregard for the law (resolved by the positive or negative response of the whole person to God's external injunction); *openness* to the grace of God versus turning away from God (resolved by the faithful or faithless response of the whole person to God's internal inspiration).

20. Come, *Human Spirit and Holy Spirit*, p. 82.

21. Ibid., p. 68.

22. Joel 2:12b, 13a.

23. *The Living Bible*, Psalm 78:36. See also Ezekiel 33:31b and Isaiah 29:13.

24. Richard J. Foster, *Celebration of Discipline: The Path to Spiritual Growth*. New York: Harper & Row, 1978. Pp. 146, 147.

25. Phillips, *The New Testament in Modern English*, Matthew 6:19a, 20a, 21, 33a.

26. Jeremiah 29:13.

27. C. S. Lewis, *Miracles: A Preliminary Study*. New York: Macmillan, 1947. Pp. 206, 207.

28. Martin Buber, *I and Thou*, trans. Walter Kaufmann. New York: Charles Scribner's Sons, 1970. P. 89.

29. Edwin Hatch, "Breathe on Me, Breath of God".

30. Ezekiel 37:1-14.

31. John 20:22.

32. Phillips, *The New Testament in Modern English*, John 14:10-12, 16-20. Italics are mine.

33. R. Laird Harris, "One View of Demon Possession", *HIS Magazine*, 1975 (March), 10.

34. The image of God is best understood not so much as something we *have*, regardless of how we *got* it, as something we *are* and *do*. The emphasis should be less on having the image of God as a collection of inherited *or* injected psychological faculties and more on imaging God, in *relationship* with Him, others, nature, and oneself. The New Testament frequently advises the believer to imitate God: love as God loves, forgive as God forgives, and be merciful as God is merciful. Our imitating or imaging God is, however, affected by the Fall, but again the emphasis should be less on substance and more on relationship. The Fall did not change our faculties from good to bad, but rather our use of them, because by inheritance from Adam we are wrongly related to God. This is not a biological inheritance (whereby *we have a sinful nature* that makes us sin), but a legal and relational inheritance (our nature is sinful because *we are sinners*). This puts justification and sanctification at the core of the matter, but whereas Christ's work regarding the former was substitutionary, the Holy Spirit's work regarding the latter is not. If it were, indwelling would be nothing more than "Christian Pantheism". (These ideas were suggested by a stimulating series on biblical anthropology, by Robert D. Brinsmead, "Man, Part 1, Part 2", *Verdict*, 1978, August, September, 6-26, 5-14).

35. Come, *Human Spirit and Holy Spirit*, pp. 115, 116.

36. Frankl, *The Unconscious God*.

37. Schaeffer, *Pollution and the Death of Man*, pp. 66, 67.

38. *The Living Bible*, Hebrews 6:1a.

39. Nels F. S. Ferré, *The Finality of Faith and Christianity Among the World Religions*. New York: Harper & Row, 1963.

40. Ibid., p. 18.

41. John Dunne, "Spiritual Adventure: The Emergence of a New Theology", *Psychology Today*, 1978 (Jan.), 47.

42. Ferré, *The Finality of Faith*, p. 15.

43. *The Living Bible*, Romans 12:12.

44. Revelation 3:20a.

45. Thomas Merton, *Contemplative Prayer*. New York: Image Books, 1971. See especially chapters 11, 15, and 19.

46. Sören Kierkegaard, *Christian Discourses*, trans. Walter Lowrie. London: Oxford University, 1940. Pp. 323, 324.

47. Matthew 7:7.

48. Alexander Dru (Ed.), *The Journals of Sören Kierkegaard*, trans. Alexander Dru. London: Oxford University, 1938. Number 572.

49. James Montgomery, "Prayer Is the Soul's Sincere Desire".

50. Jacques Ellul, *Prayer and Modern Man*, trans. C. Edward Hopkin. New York: Seabury, 1970. P. 56.

51. Romans 8:26.

52. Ellul, *Prayer and Modern Man*, p. 62.

53. Ibid., p. 60.

54. Ibid., pp. 60, 61.

Epilogue

Something more needs to be said. In a nutshell, what has already been said, and where does it all lead?

What we have in this book is a prescription for integration as living God's truth in addition to intellectually knowing about it. The whole purpose of integration is to know God, and the process of integrating is living with God. This necessarily entails, then, the Spirit-filling of both psychological and theological inquiries so they themselves can be processes of living with God. And what that involves is a pretty thorough questioning of traditional assumptions regarding the nature of the person and the nature of the Bible, and the nature of the inquiries into both.

Mechanically, the integration process is twofold. First, it involves reviewing a psychological interpretation of either God's existential or natural revelation and an apparently similar theological interpretation of God's existential or propositional revelation. The review process includes (1) verifying that each interpretation has been sufficiently demonstrated, methodologically/hermeneutically, to be true, and if they do not disagree, then (2) seeing if one of the interpretations can be subsumed by the other or recast in the other's terms (manipulation), or if they agree or are at least complementary (correlation).

Second, the integration process involves commitment to the combined idea, that is now intellectually understood to be true, in one's life over time. That is, as a framework for interpreting one's experience and/or as a guideline for making responsible choices.

Where this all leads is in a variety of directions. For one thing, the reader is encouraged to push past some of the boundaries of the typical evangelical literature, and in his or her own thinking past that which is taken for granted but not really understood. The reader is challenged to stop rehearsing safe but unproductive thoughts, to pursue the difficult and discerning rather than the easy and take-it-as-it-is. In other words, such clichés as "All truth is God's truth" and "The Bible is the final authority" must be given substance, and such mixing of categories as "Science disproves the Bible" must be debunked.

Where this has led me is into the areas of lifestyle, life planning, the Christian family, Christian counseling, and "the integration of faith and learning" in Christian education. I have seen the importance of the *context* within which the truths about each are lived out. For example, the importance of living out one's career in the context of the body of believers, while viewing one's calling as seeking first the kingdom of God and one's vocational skills as existing for service to others. Also, the importance of the context within which practitioners are trained and within which they practice, as well as the content — theory and techniques — in developing a truly Christian counseling approach.

Another excellent example of the challenge of this book is in the educational context. As a teacher of God's truth, should I embody or embalm —

give it life or preserve it? That is the choice between orthopraxy (right living) and orthodoxy (right doctrine) as the main emphasis. Although both are important, the question is which will better serve others through teaching, which will *further* the kingdom, living or preserving?[1]

It might be helpful, in conclusion, to list the steps of a living teaching process. The steps, within the framework of embodied integration, would be as follows:

1. Evaluation — initially there would need to be an evaluation of the teacher's level of expertise in the subject being taught and in the discipline of theology. Is he or she able to (1) discern how facts of interest are generated and (2) discriminate the adequacy of the methodologies involved? If the level of expertise in the subject being taught is not as high as for theology, then integration cannot proceed until the teacher attains equivalent expertise in the subject matter. Or, if the reverse is true, then further study must be done in theology.

2. Verification — if the level of expertise is roughly the same for the subject being taught and theology, the teacher would then need to verify that the facts of interest from each have been sufficiently demonstrated methodologically/hermeneutically to be true. If this is done, however, and the facts from the one disagree with the facts from the other, then integration is again irrelevant. Two "true" facts-in-contradiction call for further study and patience, not "integration".

3. Conceptual relation — if the facts have been verified and do not disagree, then a conceptual relation model would need to be chosen to bring them together into a single, combined idea.

4. Commitment and application — after conceptual relation, the teacher would commit him or herself to the authority of the combined idea in all future comparisons with related ideas. If appropriate, the teacher would also apply the idea to his or her conduct of the class. And if the combined idea holds up in practice, it thereby becomes part of the teacher's ever-growing Christian worldview.

Obviously, not all of the content of a course can be integrated, nor can all of the possible ways of conducting a class. Not all of the content of psychology and theology can be integrated, either. But quantity is not the point. Quantity is just a matter of rubbing elbows. Quality has to come from the heart . . . .

Note

1. For an excellent clarification of this issue, see C. Norman Kraus (Ed.), *Evangelicalism and Anabaptism*. Scottdale, Pennsylvania: Herald, 1979.

Author Index

Allport, Gordon, 51
Anderson, Gerald H., 57n
Argyris, Chris, 34, 40n
Arnold, W. J., 38n, 40n
Augustine, 56n

Barth, Karl, 62
Berkhof, Hendrik, 40n
Berkouwer, G. C., 55n, 56n
Bertocci, Peter A., ix, 72n
Bettis, J. D., 40n
Brinsmead, Robert D., 75n
Brunner, Heinrich Emil, 45, 54n
Bube, Richard H., 38n, 40n, 61, 73n
Buber, Martin, 62, 67, 75n
Bugental, J. F. T., 40n
Bushnell, Katherine C., 22n, 58n

Cairns, David, 54n
Calvin, John, 56n, 69
Capon, Robert Farrar, 57n
Carter, John D., 9n
Cartwright, John, 21
Cole, J. K., 40n
Coleman, Richard J., 57n
Collins, Gary R., xn, 9n
Come, Arnold B., 21n, 60, 73n, 74n, 75n
Crabb, Lawrence J., Jr., 3, 9n
Cullmann, Oscar, 74n

Doberstein, Helen, 74n
Doberstein, John, 74n
Dru, Alexander, 76n
Drury, John, 57n
Dueck, Al, xn
Dunne, John, 75n

Edie, James M., 54n
Einstein, Albert, 44, 54n
Ellul, Jacques, 39n, 71f., 76n
Evans, C. Stephen, 38n

Ferré, Nels F. S., 69, 75n, 76n
Finch, John G., 40n
Fischer, W. F., 41n

Foster, Richard J., ix, 74n
Frankl, Viktor E., 46, 55n, 69, 75n
Freud, Sigmund, 28

Gelpi, Donald L., 51, 56n
Gendlin, Eugene T., 73n
Ghiselin, E., 54n
Giorgi, Amedeo, 38n, 40n, 41n, 56n
Goethe, Johann, 18
Grounds, Vernon, 5, 9n

Hadamard, Jacques, 54n
Hardesty, Nancy, 57n
Harris, Murray, 74n
Harris, R. Laird, 75n
Harris, T. George, 38n
Harvey, John W., 22n
Hatch, Edwin, 75n
Hegel, Georg, 6
Henry, C. F. H., 21n, 74n
Heschel, Abraham, 46, 55n
Hilliard, Clarence L., 57n
Hinson, E. Glenn, 56n
Hirsch, E. D., Jr., 56n
Hodge, Charles, 55n
Hoffer, Eric, 38n
Holmer, Paul L., 56n
Holmes, Arthur F., 9n, 22n, 73n
Hopkin, C. Edward, 39n, 76n

James, William, ixn, 51
Jeeves, Malcolm A., 7, 10n
Jourard, Sidney M., 38n, 40n
Jung, Carl, 51

Kaufmann, Walter, 75n
Kelsey, Morton, 50f., 55n, 56n
Kennedy, G. A. Studdert, 38n
Kierkegaard, Sören, 17, 22n, 62, 71, 76n
Kohlberg, Lawrence, 51
Kraft, Charles H., 53, 57n, 58n
Kraus, C. Norman, 78n
Kübler-Ross, Elisabeth, 51

Laing, R. D., 35, 40n

Lake, Donald M., 73n
Lathbury, Mary Ann, 56n
Lee, A. R., 40n
Lewis, C. S., 24, 38n, 75n
Lowrie, Walter, 76n
Lunn, Brian, 74n
Luther, Martin, 69

MacKay, Donald M., 38n, 74n
Marx, Karl, 28, 53
Maslow, Abraham, 51
May, Rollo, 6, 9n, 22n, 23, 38n, 40n,
    41n, 46, 51, 55n
McLemore, Clinton W., 9n
Merleau-Ponty, Maurice, 40n, 41n, 51,
    54n
Merton, Thomas, 22n, 70, 76n
Mickelsen, Alvera, 22n
Mickelsen, Berkeley, 22n
Miskotte, K. H., 55n
Montgomery, James, 76n

Niebuhr, H. Richard, 29, 39n

Oden, Thomas C., 6, 9n
Orne, Martin T., 38n
Otto, Rudolf, 16, 22n, 54n, 55n, 74n

Page, Monte M., 22n, 38n
Paré, Amboise, 1
Phillipson, H., 40n
Piaget, Jean, 51
Pinnock, Clark, viii, xn, 39n, 40n, 57n
Polanyi, Michael, 40n

Ramm, Bernard, 55n, 57n
Reichenbach, Bruce, 62, 74n
Robertson, F. W., 54n

Rogers, Carl R., 7, 9n, 28, 51
Rogers, Jack B., 56n
Romanyshyn, Robert, 41n
Royce, Joseph R., 40n

Sanderson, William, 9n
Sands, Joshua, 57n
Sangster, W. E., 38n
Sargant, William, 9n
Schaeffer, Francis A., viii, xn, 15, 22n,
    54n, 75n
Schleiermacher, Friedrich, 16
Skinner, B. F., 24, 38n
Smith, Colin, 40n
Smith, Ronald Gregor, 22n
Sobrino, Jon, 53, 57n
Spiegelberg, Herbert, 39n
Stendahl, K., 74n
Stevens, Barry, 9n
Stransky, Thomas F., 57n

Tenney, M. C., 73n
Thielicke, Helmut, viii, xn
Thornton, L. S., 55n
Thorson, Walter R., 21n
Tournier, Paul, 41n, 55n, 74n

Von Eckartsberg, R., 41n

Wann, T. W., 38n
Warfield, Benjamin, 55n
Watts, Isaac, 54n
Wells, D. F., 56n
Wesley, John, 69
Wolfe, David L., 9n
Woodbridge, J. D., 56n

Yoder, John Howard, 40n

Subject Index

absolute certainty, 17, 27, 51

activity of the Holy Spirit, viii, 2, 5, 8, 12, 24, 25, 26, 27, 29, 30, 34, 37, 43, 44, 45, 46, 47, 50, 52, 53, 54, 56n, 59, 62, 63, 66, 68, 69, 70, 72

allegorical method, 52

alternative subcultural witnessing, 39n

Anabaptist tradition, viii, 11, 39n, 40n, 50, 57n, 77, 78, 78n

application of truth, 2, 11, 13, 17, 20, 35, 47, 50, 57n, 58n, 78

axiomatic postulation, 16, 51

bibliolatry, 47f.

body, 26, 37, 44, 45, 46, 60, 61, 62, 63, 64, 65, 66, 70

breath metaphor, 67

categories of findings, 3

changeability of soul, 61

charismania, 47, 48

Christian pantheism, 75n

coinvestigation, 33, 34f., 39n

commitment to truth, 2, 17, 18, 19, 20, 21, 35, 47, 48, 58, 77, 78

Compatibility Model, 3, 6f., 8, 28, 30

Complementarity Model, 3, 7ff., 28, 30

Comprehensive Truth, 18, 19, 20

conceptual relation, viii, 1-10, 11, 13, 14, 17, 18, 19, 20, 21, 27, 28, 29, 30, 52, 57n, 78

Conformability Model, 3, 4f., 7, 8, 12, 28, 29

consumerism, 11

contemplative orientation of emptiness, 70, 72

context, 77

Contingent Truth, 17f., 19, 20, 35

control beliefs, 4

Convertibility Model, 3, 6, 28, 30, 52

Core Model, 63, 64

correlation of findings, 3, 8, 17, 29, 77

corroboration of truth, 17, 19, 20

creation, vii, 2, 4, 5, 8, 12, 14, 15, 24, 26, 27, 28, 31, 45, 46, 55n, 61, 62, 72, 74n

Credibility Model, 3f., 5, 6, 9n, 28, 29, 47

data/discipline confusion, 3, 40n

demand characteristics, 22n, 35, 36

demon influence, 68, 75n

demythologizer, 50, 52

denying personhood, 24, 25, 43, 45, 72

developmental mysticism, 51

dialogue, 24, 34, 35, 37, 38, 39n

dichotomizer(ies), 4, 28, 31, 45, 46

dispensationalist, 50

divine sanction, 28, 52, 73n

dogmatizer(ism), 17, 27f., 29, 69

easy believism, 48

elbows together, 21, 78

embodied, viii, 2, 8, 11-22, 21, 30, 57n, 74n, 77

eschatology, 51, 52

ethical standards, vii, 5, 24, 27, 59

exclusive truth, 15, 43

Exhaustive Truth, 15f., 17, 18, 19, 22n, 43

existential revelation, 14, 15, 16, 32, 34, 43, 52, 71, 72, 77

existential validation, 33, 34, 35, 49, 50

experience as outside, 37

experiential approach, 49, 50f.

Experiential Truth, 16f., 17, 18, 19, 22n, 34, 35

experimental psychology, 7, 15, 17, 19, 20, 24, 25, 27, 31, 33, 38n, 40n, 41n

faith, 17, 62, 68, 69f., 72, 74n, 75n, 76n

fallen god view, 72, 73n

feelings, 14, 16, 17, 24, 43, 44, 45, 46, 47, 51, 52, 62, 65

feminist corrective, 53, 54

filter, 3, 4, 5

first-person perspective, 7, 15, 24, 25, 34, 35, 57n

fixation faith, 69

flesh, 23, 46, 63, 66

flexible faith, 70

fugitive faith, 70

functional authority, 47, 55n, 56n
functional control, 4, 5, 6
futile faith, 70

general revelation, 25, 32
God in the gut, 60
God's provision, 11, 46
God's truth, vii, viii, ix, 4, 5, 9n, 12, 13,
  14, 17, 18, 19, 20, 24, 25, 30, 34, 38,
  44, 48, 53, 59, 61, 66, 69, 71, 77
groanings of the Spirit, 71, 72

hardening of the categories, 18, 27, 77
hardness of heart, 46
heart, 18, 21, 23, 46, 63f., 66, 67, 68, 69,
  70, 78
hermeneutic circle, 57n
hermeneutics, 26, 52, 53, 56n, 57, 57n,
  58n, 77, 78
higher animal view, 72n, 73n
honky hermeneutic, 53, 57n
human-divine encounter, ix, 50, 51, 55n,
  56n, 59, 60, 63, 65-72
human epistemic finitude, 15
human science psychology, ix, 25, 27, 31,
  32, 39n, 40n, 48, 59
humanistic psychology, ix, 7, 15, 16, 17,
  19, 20, 25, 40n
humanistic theology, 16, 17, 19, 20, 31,
  32, 48
humanness, 12f., 24, 25, 34, 37, 43, 44,
  46, 52, 59, 60, 71

identity of disciplines, 1, 2, 3, 4, 9, 14,
  28, 29
image of God, 68, 75n
immaculate perception, 14, 44
immortality, 45, 62, 74n
in-here/out-there problem, vii, viii, ix, 16,
  17
indwelling, 67ff., 74n
integration as a starting point, 48
intentionality, 37, 44, 60, 61, 62, 65, 70
interexperience, 35, 36, 37
intolerance of ambiguity, 27
intuition, 16, 25, 51

kingdom of God, viii, ix, 20, 39n, 57n,
  58n, 65, 70, 77

knowing God, viii, 12, 13, 14, 16, 17, 43,
  44, 51, 57n, 66, 77
knowing truth, 13-21, 44, 47, 56n, 60
knowledge of good and evil, 44

Layer Model, 63, 64
legitimizer, 29, 59
levels of inquiry, 31, 33, 49
liberation theology, 53, 54, 57n, 58n
lifestyle, 39n, 77
literal/liberal conflict, 52, 57n
lived experience, 7, 24, 34, 38, 43, 57, 60
living out, viii, 2, 11, 13, 17, 20, 26, 35,
  47, 48, 57, 58n, 72, 77
living with God, vii, ix, 12, 13, 20, 43, 48,
  55n, 59, 62, 74n, 77

manipulation of findings, viii, 2, 3, 5, 6,
  17, 28, 29, 77
meanings, 16, 24, 25, 26, 31, 33, 34, 35,
  37f., 40n, 41n, 52, 55n, 56n, 60, 61
men without chests, 24
methodological flow chart, 48, 49
methods dictating questions, 27, 38
mind, 26, 43, 44, 46, 50, 53, 60f., 62, 63,
  64, 65, 66, 73n
mixing of categories, 3, 9n, 40n, 77
multi-perspectival method, 53f., 57n, 59
mystery, 16, 25, 27, 43, 55n, 56n, 57n,
  58n, 67
mythological method, 52

natural revelation, 14, 15, 32, 34, 71, 77
natural science method, 14, 15, 25, 51
natural science psychology, 24, 25, 31, 32
nature of the Bible, ix, 55n, 77
nonrational, 16, 22n, 55n

orthopraxy, 53, 57n, 58n, 78

paper Gospel, 5, 48
parameters for knowing truth, 14f.
peace that passes understanding, 17, 22n
perfect integration, 28
phenomenal worlds, 16, 31, 32, 33, 34,
  44, 49, 60, 62, 70
phenomenological approach, ix, 17, 31,
  33, 34, 37, 38n, 39n, 40n, 41n, 51,
  54n, 56n

philological method, 52
platonic thinking, 45f., 63, 74n
powers and principalities, 39n, 40n, 58n
prayer(ful), 14, 24, 37, 46, 48, 51, 69, 70ff., 76n
primacy of perception, 44, 47, 48, 52, 54n
primal bottom, 16
process/product distinction, 1, 2, 5, 18, 48, 54, 57n, 58n, 77, 78
professional orthodoxy, 30
propositional revelation, 14, 15, 32, 34, 44, 47, 52, 53, 66, 71, 72, 77
psychological imperialism, 3, 6
psychological methodology, vii, ix, 2, 5, 8, 12, 18, 24, 25, 30-38, 40n, 44, 66, 72, 77
psychotheology, 31

rationalism, 16, 45, 50, 55n
rearranging the revelation, 28
reciprocal observation, 34
reconstruction variation, ix, 5, 12, 27
re-creation hypothesis, 62
regenerate person, 67
reification hypothesis, 62
reinterpretation variation, 5
relationship metaphor, 67f.
religiofication, 28
religious experience, ixn, 6, 14, 16, 32, 43, 44, 46, 47, 48, 50, 51, 52, 56n
restricting personhood, 43, 44, 45, 72

scientific theology, 15, 17, 19, 20, 31, 32, 48, 51
secular/sacred conflict, 3, 4, 29, 30, 45
songs from my life, 20, 21
soul, 23, 26, 45, 46, 53, 60, 61f., 63, 65, 66, 71

special revelation, 25, 32
spirit, 12, 13, 21n, 45, 46, 59, 60, 62f., 65, 66, 67, 72n, 73n, 74n, 75n
Spirit-filled psychology, ix, 12, 27, 29, 30, 34, 37, 59, 65, 66, 67, 68, 72, 77
Spirit-filled theology, 44, 59, 65, 66, 67, 68 72, 77
synthesizer(sis), 7, 28, 62
systematic integration, 1, 18, 19, 20, 78
systems theory, 61f.

theological imperialism, 3
theological methodology, 2, 8, 12, 15, 18, 26, 30, 44, 50, 51, 57n, 66
transactional approach, 49, 50, 51f.
transactionalism, 56n
translator's consciousness, 14, 20, 31, 52, 53, 54
truth as framework and guide, 13, 17, 77
truth for me, 13, 17, 18, 19, 20, 35, 47, 48
types of truth, 15-21
typological method, 52

Unity Model, 63, 64

verification of method, 2, 15, 20, 48, 57n, 77, 78

wait on the Lord, 20, 71
well-designed experiment, 24
wholehearted worship, 65
whole person, 38n, 44, 45, 46f., 48, 52, 59, 60, 61, 62, 63, 65, 67, 70, 71, 72n, 74n
will, ix, 22n, 40n, 41n, 46, 55n, 61, 63, 67, 71, 72n, 73n
worldview, 1, 2, 4f., 18, 40n, 78